PEOPLE I WANT TO PUNCH IN THE THROAT

VOLUMES 1 - 6

JEN MANN

THROAT PUNCH MEDIA, LLC

For everyone who needs a laugh.

All of the names and identifying characteristics of the people who appear in this book have been changed to protect the bad, the good, and the ugly. So if you think you see yourself in these pages, please be assured that you are almost certainly wrong. These are my stories and this is how I remember them.

INTRODUCTION

Hi there, I'm Jen. I'm assuming that if you're reading this book, you already know that. I can't imagine that anyone except my mom and maybe a handful of the die hard fans of my blog People I Want to Punch in the Throat would read this, so I'm not sure why I'm writing an introduction. I figure that anyone who got this book already knows me and what I'm all about.

Wait. You don't know who I am? You're just sitting in a carpool line or in your cubicle at lunch time with your egg salad sandwich and you've never heard of me or my writings before? Well, then! Pull up a chair and let me tell you a little bit about myself.

I'm a sarcastic, sweary, hysterical, sometimes offensive, middle-aged, exhausted, married, mother of two who tends to say out loud what everyone else is thinking. One of my friends actually called my writing "brilliantly acerbic with a surprising warmth." I couldn't write a better description—that sums me up perfectly—so now I just use that description everywhere!

I have two kids: Gomer (aged 14) and Adolpha (aged

12). Before you have a coronary and pull out your embossed stationary to write me a nasty letter about my horrible taste in names, just stop, because you're an idiot. *Of course*, those aren't their real names.

Their real names are actually worse, but I can't take the ridicule.

If you still feel strongly, go ahead and write me a letter. Hate readers are my favorites.

I call my husband The Hubs. It annoys the hell out of lots of people, so I keep doing it. His name isn't important, you can call him The Hubs too. Everyone does. He's a cheap bastard who can be a tad anti-social, but he treats me like gold, so he's my lobster. Oh yeah, he's Chinese and I'm Caucasian, sometimes that information is good to know when you're reading my stuff.

I've lived in Iowa, New Jersey, Illinois, Kansas, and New York. I currently live in Kansas. It doesn't blow as much as you'd think it would. I don't live on a farm or anything like that. I live in a suburb with gun-toting competi-moms, douchey dads, McMansions, and award-winning schools. It's like its own circle of hell, but with Targets and Starbucks on every corner—and a few of our Targets have Starbucks INSIDE of them (a sure sign of the impending Apocalypse).

My mom is a certified overachiever who mastered the fine art of housekeeping. That woman gave me a white glove test every week before I could go out with my friends and actually *combed* our stairs. In return for ironing his undershirts, my dad is her Sugar Daddy who keeps her outfitted in fancy vacuums and pays her Chico's bill without question. Hey, it's a good gig if you can get it.

I moved around a lot as a kid. My dad had one of those corporate jobs where they test your loyalty by making you move every couple of years to an even worse place than where you started. Because we moved so often, I never got to have a bright pink bedroom or hang pictures on my walls. My parents insisted that my bedroom be a neutral color, thus no need to repaint and they were convinced that every nail hole brought down their house's resale value by the thousands.

You would think that moving all the time would have made me an outgoing kid, but it didn't. I hated standing up in the front of a new class and being introduced on my first day. I hated when the teacher would ask, "Who will have lunch with Jenni today?" But what I hated worse was moving in middle school and high school when teachers didn't set up lunch dates for you anymore. I didn't find my voice until college. That's when I changed my name to "Jen," because it's soooo much cooler than Jenni with an adorable "i" and that's when I started saying whatever was on my mind. By the time I hit my thirties I had no more fucks to give.

This is a collection of original essays about what makes me tick and what makes me Jen. These essays and stories can't be found anywhere else. Not on my blog and not in my other books. Just here!

This is a compilation of the first six volumes. Each volume is different and you never know what you'll find. They are an assortment of my childhood memories, stories about my kids and the Hubs, and rants about everything that make me punchy all told with my usual snarky take.

I think the stories I tell are mostly true. You know how you remember an event one way and another person remembers it another? I'm sure there's some of that in here, but I'm not going to worry about that. If they have a problem, they can write their own damn story!

CHAPTER 1

SARAH: THE FIRST PERSON I EVER WANTED TO PUNCH IN THE THROAT

WHEN I WAS four years old, I was given the worst news I could have ever imagined: my mother was pregnant. I was devastated and pissed all at the same time. I'd had four years of undivided attention where I was the center of the universe. I never had to share, I never had to compromise and now suddenly, I was supposed to be excited about the prospect of some smelly, wailing thing coming into my life?

I couldn't understand why my parents had made this decision. I had never given them any indication that I was interested in having a sibling. I was the perfect only child. I was docile and obedient. I was precocious and adorable. Why would they want to take a chance? Who knew what we might get? This was my first realization that my parents were not very bright—an opinion that I would hold firmly for the next ten years or so.

When my mother told me I was going to be a big sister, I exclaimed, "Whose idea was this anyway? Certainly not mine!" Yeah, I was mouthy even back then.

Trying to make me feel better, my mother quickly assured me that she was carrying a girl. My dad looked horrified. It was if I could read his mind: *Drats, another girl!?*

"How do you know that?" he asked. He looked at her like she was a fortune teller at a carnival, because remember, this was the seventies. There were no ultrasound looky-loos for "turtles." You had to wait for the doctor to actually see a penis or a vagina on the screaming baby he was catching before you knew the sex.

"I just have a feeling," she smiled at me. I smiled back. A baby in general sounded horrible, but I figured a baby *sister* didn't sound *that* bad.

"You're sure?" I asked, slowly warming up to the idea of sharing my space with an obnoxious entity.

"I. Promise."

I promise. Whoa. My mother didn't take promises lightly and neither did I. After that, my mother and I started calling the baby in her belly "Sarah." We talked about Sarah all the time.

"Do you think Sarah will look like me?" I asked my mother as she braided my hair in the mornings.

"I sure hope so," she replied.

"Do you think Sarah will want to ride a bike with me?" I yelled as I winged my hot pink Huffy around our cul-de-sac.

"When she's bigger she will."

"Can Sarah and I have bunkbeds and share a room?" I asked after my bedtime story.

"Probably."

Sarah, Sarah, Sarah. I was starting to get excited now. *Sarah, Sarah, Sarah.*

Because I was four, I didn't understand the tense conversations my parents would have when they thought I was watching *Scooby Doo.*

"You do know there's a good chance this baby is a boy?" my father asked my mother one Saturday morning.

She glanced at me to see if I'd heard, but I continued to stuff my face with Lucky Charms and dream of being Velma. (By the way, who the hell dreams of being Velma? This girl. I wanted glasses desperately and I think deep down even at four years old, I knew I'd never be the "hot" one, so I might as well reach for something I could actually accomplish.)

"Shhh ... Jenni will hear you!"

"Okay. Maybe she should. The baby is due in a couple of weeks and the two of you are calling it 'Sarah' all the time. What happens if it's a 'Sam'?"

"It won't be. I can tell. I feel the same way I did when I was pregnant with Jenni. It's a girl. I'm certain of it! And besides, I *hate* the name Sam, so no matter what, this baby will *never* be called 'Sam.'"

"Uh huh. Well, if this thing goes poorly, *you're* the one who's dealing with Jenni, because I don't want to hear it. She will be a nightmare if the baby is a boy—and *you* created that nightmare. And, by the way, what's wrong with Sam? I think that's a good strong name!"

"I've got three words for you: 'Sam I am' and before you even say it, Sammy is completely worse. It's not on the list. *At all.*"

The next day, my mother took me into the yellow gender neutral nursery next door to my room and showed me two outfits she had hanging in the closet. One was a pink dress for Sarah and the other was some ugly blue sailor suit I assumed she bought for a neighbor's baby.

"Jenni," my mother said. "the baby will be here soon."

"Yup. Sarah is coming."

"Right. So ... I'm pretty sure the baby is a girl, but there is a teeny, weeny, itsy, bitsy chance it will be a boy."

"What? No. You promised me a sister."

"I know I did. And I *feel* like this is a girl. I do! But ... babies can be girls or boys and you just never know what you're going to get."

"We're getting a girl," I said, stomping my little foot.

"We don't know what we're going to get."

"It. Is. A. Girl." I clenched my tiny fists.

"We. Don't. Know," my mother said in that soft and deadly voice parents use when they're trying very hard not to beat the shit out of you.

"You broke your promise."

"I didn't. I haven't ... Not yet at least," she muttered.

"What?"

"Umm, nevermind. Let's just change the subject," my mother said trying to divert me. There was only one thing that could take my mind off of the horrible news that I might be getting a brother instead of a sister. "Guess what! Grandma is coming to stay with you while I'm in the hospital. Won't that be fun?"

"Uh huh," I said suspiciously. I was four, but I wasn't an idiot. I knew she was trying to bribe me with extra Grandma time.

"She'll be here the whole week I'm in the hospital." You gotta love 1970s health care where you got a whole week in the hospital for having a baby! "I bet she'll take you to do some really super fun things!"

"Maybe," I said shrugging. I couldn't be swayed so easily. "Like what?"

"Like ... the park ... and maybe the zoo ... or swimming .... or out to a big girl lunch, because now you'll be mommy's helper. The big sister."

I refused to be led astray. "A big sister to a little sister," I insisted.

My mother sighed heavily. "Look, Jenni, I'm sorry I promised you. I shouldn't have done that. I have no control over what we get. It will be a surprise. When the baby comes then we'll *all* know, won't we?"

"Sarah is coming."

"We'll see. But either way, you'll have a very important job to do."

My ears perked up at the word "job." It's probably the bossiness in me, but I've always been a sucker for a job and a title. It didn't matter if my job was simply to make sure all of the lights were off in the kitchen after dinner, if you gave me a good job description and called me The Official Kitchen Light Extinguisher, I would do that job better than anyone else. I wanted a job. "What kind of job?"

"Well, the most important job you'll have is to make sure Grandma brings the right outfit to the hospital for the new baby."

"That's easy. We'll bring the pink dress for Sarah."

"Um ... Daddy will call and tell Grandma if it's a girl *or a boy* and then you'll get the right outfit out of the closet for the baby. That's a very important job, isn't it?" My mother asked me like I had a brain injury.

At this point, reality started to sink in and I saw that things might not go my way as far as getting a sister. As badly as I wanted to bring that pink dress to the hospital, I was beginning to understand that my mother couldn't keep her promise to me. I was devastated. However, I knew that if I played my cards right I could get reparations. I saw my opportunity and I took it. "I'll take that job. But I need new crayons," I said.

My mother narrowed her eyes. "What's wrong with the crayons you have?"

"I don't like them anymore. They're not sharp. The baby can have them. I need new ones."

My mother studied me for a moment. She knew the odds of her bringing home a sister and keeping her promise were fifty-fifty. She knew she'd over-promised, but she saw that she could get out of breaking her promise fairly easily. "Fine."

"I want the big box with the built in sharpener," I negotiated. "And a new coloring book."

"Done," my mother agreed. "We'll go to the store tomorrow."

Only we didn't go to the store the next day, because that night Sarah arrived.

Only her name wasn't Sarah.

His name was C.B. and he was the first person I ever wanted to punch in the throat.

CHAPTER 2

TODAY I AM A WOMAN. OH
SHUT THE FUCK UP, WILL YA?

I BECAME A WOMAN AT THIRTEEN. No, I didn't get boobs. I'd had those since I was about nine or ten. (By the way, boobs at nine *totally* sucks.) At thirteen I got my period. Like all girls in the eighties I'd read the "manual" on becoming a woman: Judy Blume's *Are You There God? It's Me, Margaret.* Judy educated all of us on the magical and mystical journey that was our menses. Only Judy's book was written in the early seventies when there were things called "belted sanitary napkins." I can't tell you how much this term confused and worried me. I imagined a real belt, preferably a braided leather one, around my waist with some sort of cloth napkin (like the ones my mother used at holiday dinners, maybe?) attached to it. I've since discovered that the newer editions of the book changed this contraption to an adhesive maxi pad. Soooo much easier to understand!

When Margaret got her period it was kind of a big deal. Her mom helped her figure out her belt thingy and told her she was growing up or something inspiring and bonding-*ish* like that. I sort of envisioned my mother-daughter experience would be like that. Boy, was I wrong.

My friends and I were fairly private about the whole Aunt Flo thing. I wasn't sure who had had a visit and who hadn't. I don't remember feeling a particular angst over it, but I do remember wanting to just get it over with.

I wish my friends (and Judy Blume) had told me a bit more about what to expect though. For instance, they could have mentioned that the first time you ever get your period the blood might not be red. Yeah. It can be brown. And it can look a lot like some bizarre diarrhea or something. Thanks a lot, Judy. That info would have been helpful, because when I got my period for the first time it looked nothing like blood. It looked like I took a dump in my undies.

The timing totally sucked, because I got my period on the day we were moving. Once again. By this time I had lost count of how many times we'd moved, but it was a lot. Before I was born, my dad had grand ideas of being a semi-professional student for the rest of his life. Or at least a college professor. He imagined a future full of tweed and elbow patches and summers off to write. I screwed that up, because my parents had me when they were ridiculously young. Like too young to be having kids, but totally old enough because this was the seventies, man, and there was a war going on and that made people mature faster, and blah, blah, blah. (Meanwhile, there was a war going on when *I* was twenty as well, and it didn't give *me* the desire and maturity to marry a guy and have babies, but whatever.) Anyway, babies cost money and professional students don't make much, so once I arrived, graduate school went in the crapper. My dad had to take one of those corporate jobs where they test your loyalty by making you move every couple of years to an even worse city than where you started. We'd been in our cookie cutter tract home for eighteen months, so it was time to move again to another cookie cutter tract home that would be easy to resell in another eighteen months as long as we didn't get wild with the paint colors. I never got to have a pink bedroom growing up. They always had to be a shade of white, because white is easy to sell. So my bedroom was always White Heron, Bone White, Moonlight White, Atrium White, or Linen White. Guess what color I don't have in my house now? White.

The day I got my period, the movers were at our house all day and my mother was a psychotic cleaning whirling dervish following behind them, scouring every surface until it shone. On a normal day, that woman was an insane cleaning machine. She gave me and C.B. a white glove test every Friday and actually *combed* the carpet on our staircase. She was always vacuuming. (I swear, the most vivid memory I have of my whole childhood is my mother either vacuuming, putting away the vacuum, or the vacuum sitting in the middle of the front hall waiting to be used and/or put away—I think that's why I despise vacuuming to this day.) If she was crazy on a normal day, she was certifiable on moving days. We were moving thousands of miles away and yet she still worried what the new owners might tell our old neighbors about the dust bunnies we left behind. So she followed the movers, cleaning everything in their wake. She dusted blinds, washed bathroom cabinets, swept the attic, and weeded the flower beds before she handed over the keys to the front door to the Realtor. Now that I'm a Realtor, I understand why she did that. I may never see those dirty sellers again, but I do judge them. And I don't forget them. I am shocked and appalled by the horrid state that some people leave an empty house in. My mother is a bit extreme, but you *could* vacuum when you move out your filthy couch, asshole.

My mom couldn't accomplish her numerous tasks with C.B. and I underfoot, so she sent us away for the day. I ended up at the mall with a friend and her mother, Mrs. Anderson. About an hour into our shopping I was overcome with horrible stabbing stomach pains. Mrs. Anderson was concerned and had us sit down. That's when she noticed that my white shorts were stained brown. (Seriously, could I have worse luck? Who the hell gets their first period at the mall in a pair of white shorts? This girl.) "Jenni, are you feeling all right? It looks like you've had ... an accident," Mrs. Anderson asked me.

I looked down at my ruined shorts. "Oh my God! What is wrong with me??"

"It looks like you need to go to the bathroom," my friend said. *Ya think, Einstein?*

I ran to the bathroom and discovered an even bigger mess inside my shorts. "Holy shit," I said.

"Excuse me?!" the old lady in the next stall said. "Watch your language, young lady!"

"Sorry, but I think I'm dying!" I yelled back.

"I doubt that. Give it some time and it will come."

"What are you talking about?" I cried.

"Constipation. Sometimes it can feel like you're dying," the old lady said.

Ewww! Stop giving me advice on my bowels, old lady! "Oh my God! I'm having the opposite of constipation!" I wailed.

"Jenni?" Now it was Mrs. Anderson coming into the bathroom. "I bought you a new pair of shorts and underwear."

"Oh ,thank you!" I said, gratefully.

"It's fine. Your mother can pay me back when I take you home."

Let me just stop my story right here. On the one hand, I think it was very thoughtful of this woman to go out and buy me new underwear and shorts, but on the other hand, she's going to ask to be reimbursed? *Really?* As I sat on that toilet surveying the damage in my pants, I swore right then and there that if I was ever an adult around a young kid who accidentally shit his or her pants (because at this point, that's what I thought had happened) I would do what ever I could to ease the almost paralyzing embarrassment that kid must feel, including, but not limited to, never asking their parent to reimburse me for new underwear and shorts! *You know what, kid? That change of clothes is on me!*

"I think you should change your clothes and we should take you home."

"Okay," I mumbled as I cleaned up myself and put on my new panties and shorts.

Mrs. Anderson made me sit with a wad of TP crammed in my drawers on an old towel she found in the trunk of her car. "I'm sorry dear, but Mr. Anderson just had the car detailed."

When my mother met us at the door with a harried expression and the vacuum, I knew it wasn't going to go well. "Why are you home, already?" she demanded, looking at her watch and calculating that she still had at least two hours to clean baseboards before I was due back.

"Jenni had ... an accident," Mrs. Anderson said.

"What kind of accident? Are you hurt?" my mother asked, dropping her vacuum, suddenly concerned.

"No. Nothing like that. She ... messed her pants."

"*What?* You did what?"

I started crying. "I don't know how it happened. I felt sick and then all of a sudden my pants were ruined."

She looked me up and down, "They don't look ruined."

"Well, that's because I bought her new ones," said Mrs. Anderson.

"Oh. Well. Thank you for that."

"Yes, well, actually they cost about fifteen dollars. So ..."

"So ..." my mother challenged. My mother would have totally said, *The new outfit is on me, kid!*

"Well ... she needed new underwear and shorts, so I went to Macy's."

"Macy's? No wonder it cost you fifteen dollars! Who shops for kids at Macy's?"

"It was the closest store ... There wasn't a lot of choice," Mrs. Anderson said imperiously.

My mother backed down a hair. "You know what? You're right. I'm sorry. Thank you for taking care of her. Did you want fifteen bucks?"

"Well ... yes. That would be nice."

"Jenni, go and get my wallet. I have a twenty in there. I was going to use it get some pizza for us and the movers for dinner tonight, but this is more important. Don't you think, Mrs. Anderson?" She looked Mrs. Anderson straight in the eye. My mother could teach a whole course on passive aggressive manipulation.

Mrs. Anderson backed down. "Um ... you know what? Keep it. It's fine. I'm happy to do it. Think of the new clothes as a going away present for, Jenni."

"Oh! That's wonderful. Thank you so much. What do you say, Jenni?" my mother asked.

"Thank you," I mumbled weakly. *Just what I wanted! Terry cloth shorts! I'll treasure them!*

As my mom shut the door on Mrs. Anderson, she rounded on me, "What happened? You pooped your pants in the middle of the mall?"

"I guess so. I don't know," I whined.

"Go and take a shower. There are still towels in the hall bath, but you'll have to clean the tub when you're done. I've already cleaned that bathroom because we're moving to the hotel tonight."

I went into the bathroom and inspected the underwear Mrs. Anderson had purchased. Now the brown had been replaced with bright red. Suddenly, a light bulb went on in my dim brain. "Mom!" I screamed.

"What?" my mother ran into the bathroom. "What's wrong?"

"I didn't poop my pants! I got my *period*!"

I waited for my mom to whoop or laugh or cry or *something*. She just stared at me. "Well, I suppose that's good. At least you're not sick or something."

"It's just that I'm a ... woman now."

"Uh huh. That's great. I'm thrilled for you," my mom said, obviously less than thrilled. Of course she wasn't thrilled. A woman's period isn't called the "curse" for nothing. Who wants to bleed every month and feel like shit? No one.

"Wow. Cramps suck, huh?" I said, speaking from my three minutes experience of being a menstruating woman. "*So much* worse than gas pains."

"Jenni, do you have any idea how much I have to do today?" my mom asked me wearily. "I have so much work to do and I don't know how I'm going to get it all done. I haven't even started wiping down the kitchen cupboards."

"Okay, but ..."

"But what?" my mother asked impatiently.

It wasn't like I wanted a fucking Period Party (which, by the way, that shit actually exists, go Google it and prepare to be horrified), but a "I hear ya, sister" on the cramps thing, and a high five would have been cool. Plus, I had no idea what to *do* exactly. I didn't have a belt and my mom had packed all of our napkins, so ... was I just supposed to walk around with a bunch of toilet paper clutched between my legs for the next five to seven days?

"Well, what do I do?"

"*Do?*"

"What do I use ..."

"Oh God. Didn't they teach you about this in Health class?"

"Sorta. I don't remember." I was probably reading another Judy Blume book under the desk and missed that part.

"Hold on. I've packed everything, but I might have something in my purse. Lesson number one: you never know when you'll get your period, so always keep supplies handy."

A few minutes she came back with a box of super-duper-mega absorbent tampons. Compared to my thirteen-year-old vagina they looked about the size of a cucumber.

"What do I do with these?"

My mother looked incredibly uncomfortable. "The instructions are in the box," she explained. "Oh. And you might need this to help you ... see what you're doing." She handed me a small hand mirror.

"I'll be in the kitchen. Come find me when you're finished. I can give you a Tylenol and put you to work."

She left me sitting on the edge of the tub with the box of massive tampons and the hand mirror.

What the actual fuck?

I got out the instructions and started reading about Toxic Shock Syndrome. Holy crap, maybe stuffing wads of toilet paper in my crotch *would* be better! I studied the diagram showing the various holes in my body and the proper way to hold the enormous cotton plug, but it didn't help.

I destroyed at least five tampons that day.

The first one, I took the applicator off BEFORE trying to insert it. I worked really hard on another one until I realized I was trying to jam it up my asshole. Three more died a slow painful death from simply being over-handled and mauled while I kept trying to wedge them into a hole that was way too small. The mirror was absolutely no help, because for the life of me, I couldn't make heads or tails of my orifices (thus the tampon up the ass). I started crying from sheer exhaustion and embarrassment.

"Jenni?" It was my mother knocking on the door. "How you doing in there? Everything going okay?"

"No! I need help. I don't know how to do this!" I yelled back.

She opened the door. "Well, I don't know what you want from me," she said exasperated. My mom is a great mom and loves us dearly, but when you need her during a time of crisis or, God forbid, the dead of the night, she's worthless. Once, when I was a kid and got up for a pre-dawn session of puking and cried for her, she came, but then quickly declared that there wasn't much she could do to help me, so she was going to go ahead and get back to sleep. Now that I'm a mother, I completely get that. Middle of the night barfing is the worst, because as long as the kid is getting it in the toilet, what can you do except feel pissed off because your warm bed is missing you?

"I need you ... to put it in," I sobbed.

My mother looked horrified. "Absolutely not. I can't do that."

"Well, I can't do it!"

"Did you use the mirror? And the instructions?"

"Yes! They both suck! I can't figure it out. I need the belted sanitary napkins!"

"The what?"

"It's a belt with napkins you attach."

"I know exactly what it is, but how do *you*? They haven't made those in years."

"I read about them in a book. Judy Blume never mentioned a thing that goes inside of you. I need the napkins!"

"Well, I don't have those. We'd have to go to the store and—"

"Yes! I know! You don't have time!" I screamed.

"Jenni! Calm down," she soothed me. "It's going to be fine. You can do this."

"I can't! You think it's terrible that I'm asking you to help me insert a tampon, but how do you think I feel? I just had to ask my mother to put a tampon inside me!"

"I don't understand the problem. Why can't you just use the mirror? Everyone just fumbles through the first few times. Keep trying. You'll get it."

She left me sitting on the toilet crying until my legs were numb. There was a soft knock at the door. "Jenni?" It was my dad. "Your mom is cleaning ceiling fans and she says you need to go to the store. I'm worthless at cleaning, but I can drive you to the pharmacy."

Oh shit. My dad? Are you kidding me?

I took another look at my mother's enormous tampons. It couldn't be any worse shopping with my dad for feminine products. *Fine.*

I jammed my panties full of Kleenex and hopped in the car with my dad.

It was like some bad sitcom. My dad lurked at the far end of the "Feminine Hygiene" aisle where he took a great interest in an endcap of hearing aid batteries while I scoured through the vast assortment of pads. (I completely skipped the tampon section. I was too traumatized to even peruse those shelves. It would take me another several years to figure out that tampons come in slim sizes and work well for the less vaginally endowed.)

"Dad?"

"Yup!" he looked up from the sympathy card he was reading intently.

"What are the wings for? Do I need wings?" I asked.

"Umm ... I haven't a clue. Maybe ask the pharmacist." The pharmacist was seventy-year-old man. No thanks. I'd had enough embarrassment for the day.

"What about deodorant or scented? Which one should I get?"

Dad looked up from the shelf of Ben-Gay that he was straightening, "I have no clue, Jenni! Why don't you pick a bunch and you can try them all at home and see what you like best?"

"Dad, what are panty liners?"

"Jenni!" My dad slammed a bottle of foot powder on the shelf. "Pick something. *Please.*"

I went up to the register with about a hundred bucks worth of adhesive (no belt, thank God!) sanitary napkins: super absorbent over-nighters with wrap around wings, lightweight ultra-thin ones without wings, deodorized and/or scented ones with dri-weave technology, a box of super longs (that covered me from belly button to butt crack), and some panty liners. My dad gave me his credit card and waited for me in the car.

I know my mom was busy that day and that last thing she needed was for my lady days to fuck up her moving schedule, BUT my mom has always been uncomfortable talking to me about anything "bodily" so I'm not sure it would have gone any differently if it hadn't been moving day. When my mom tried to tell me about the birds and the bees she checked out a book from the library about pregnant animals. The photograph showing hundreds of eggs in the belly of the dissected pregnant fish still haunts me. "But you only have one in there, right?" I asked nervously, rubbing my mother's burgeoning belly. "Of course! What did you think?"

I don't know! You're the one showing me a dead and dissected pregnant fish full of dead eggs, woman!

I made two promises that day: one—I would never ask to be reimbursed when a young girl needs new clothes due to a mortifying event, and two—when it is Adolpha's turn to receive the curse of womanhood I will help her and guide her, and if necessary, I will insert a tampon for her (even if it's moving day), because pads really suck balls—especially the ones with wings.

CHAPTER 3

"WEAR YOUR DAMN COAT" AND OTHER THINGS I'D LIKE TO SAY TO YOUR KID

I WAS at a potential real estate client's house early one winter morning. The owners, Carl and Melanie, were both working parents with hectic schedules. Evenings and weekends were full of extracurricular activities for the kids so they'd asked me to have an early morning meeting with them before they left for the day. When I rang the bell, Melanie met me at the door with her wet hair wrapped in a towel and a piece of toast in her hand.

"Hi!" she exclaimed. "Welcome to our morning madness. Come on in."

I don't know what the evenings and weekends are like, but I could quickly tell that morning was a terrible time of day for a meeting with these two. They were trying to get ready for work, get the dog walked, get their kids fed and out the door to school on time, all while they tried to find some time to sit down and tell me how old the roof and furnace were, if the swing set in the backyard stayed, and if they were at all negotiable on price.

Melanie finished feeding the dog and joined me in the living room so we could talk.

"How long have you lived here?" I asked Melanie.

"Hmm," she thought for a moment. "we moved in the year before Sanderson was born, so four years."

"Okay." I made a note in my file. "Are you the first owners?"

Melanie nodded and then yelled, "Carl! Don't forget to put Braxtyn's tae kwon do uniform in the car! There won't be time to come home from Y-care and get it. Sorry, Jen. What was the question?"

Carl interrupted us. "I can't find the uniform and Sanderson just dumped the dog's water bowl on his head. I'm going to need some help."

Melanie hopped up. "Excuse me, Jen. Carl, you change Sanderson and then help me look for the uniform. We've got to find it. Braxtyn is testing for her yellow belt today and Mr. Han won't promote her in sweat pants!"

I was left alone with the dog staring at me. I couldn't be sure, but he looked thirsty to me. "Don't look at me," I said to the dog. "Go lick Sanderson." I wanted to say, *Hey Melanie, maybe your kid could skip a tae kwon do lesson this week so you could get your house on the market? What's more important? Your precious snowflake's yellow belt test or getting your biggest investment sold?*

I sighed heavily and stood up from the couch. I did what I could on my own. I peeked in closets, took note of the upgraded countertops in the kitchen, and the new tile in the bathroom. I figured the square footage and determined the market value for the home. I even found the tae kwon do uniform shoved in the hall closet when I was doing my walk through. I was ready to get contracts signed and be on my way.

The problem was, Carl and Melanie were far too busy wrangling kids and the dog to give me a minute or two.

"Jen," Carl said. "come on out to the kitchen and we can talk while the kids eat breakfast."

I sat down at the table and tried to give my best sales pitch of why I was the only Realtor for the job while the three-year-old threw oatmeal at me. I tried to wow them with my stats while the dog was told repeatedly to stop humping my leg. Apparently the dog has rules, but the kid doesn't.

I was exhausted at my wits end when I finally got my paperwork signed. I was packing up so I could get the hell out of there when five-year-old Braxtyn announced she wouldn't be wearing a coat that day. Both of her parents looked at one another and sort of shrugged their shoulders.

"Well, Braxtyn," Melanie said. "that is entirely your choice. However, your decision might result in a consequence for you."

I stopped shuffling my papers. *A consequence. Ugh.*

Nothing makes me cringe more than hearing a parent simper those two words. That just means that there will be a ridiculous drawn out discussion for the next twenty minutes about good choices and bad choices instead of a parent just manning the fuck up and telling their kid to do something, dammit.

Before I knew what I was doing, I was chiming in with my two cents. "Oh, Braxtyn! I've been out already this morning. It's freezing out there! You need to wear a coat."

"No I don't," Braxtyn said, pouting.

"Braxtyn can make her choice as long as she understands that there are consequences to her actions," Melanie said.

Are you kidding me with this?

Melanie continued, "For instance, Braxtyn, you might end up at the doctor's office."

"Uh-oh!" exclaimed Carl widening his eyes in pretend pain and fear. "Not the doctor's office!"

Are you a grown ass man or a cartoon character who just got hit in the balls with a wooden mallet?

I couldn't keep my mouth shut. Again. "Well, that's not really a consequence for Braxtyn. *You're* the one who has to take the day off of work to care for a sick kid. *You're* the one who has to pay the doctor's bill. That's not a consequence for Braxtyn and she has no understanding of what her decision has actually done to *you*."

Melanie and Carl looked at me like I'd just exposed my left breast at their kitchen table. The look they gave me was a combination of revulsion and intrigue. My breasts have that kind of power over people, so I double checked to make sure my shirt was, in fact, still buttoned.

The Girls were securely locked down; it must have been what I said.

Shit. Shut. The. Fuck. Up. Jen. Why must you speak? Why? They signed the papers. You are here to sell their house, not go all Super Nanny on them.

"So, what are you suggesting exactly, Jen?" Carl asked. "Just tell her to wear her coat and that's the end of the discussion?"

I blurted out, "Yes. It's a no-brainer."

OHMYGODSHUT UP. This is a good listing, you idiot. It will sell fast and for asking price and then they will love you and they will send you all of their friends and family. They are not interested in having you drop nuggets of unwanted parenting wisdom on them.

Carl tried to drop some of his own parenting wisdom he obviously gleaned from some bullshit parenting book he received from someone who obviously hates him and wants his children to grow up to be demon spawn. "Jen, children need to be able to make decisions for themselves or else they feel out of control," he said.

"Sure," I said. "I agree. Let her make decisions that don't matter. Let her choose if she wants braids or a pony tail in her hair. Let her choose if she wants to wear a pink dress or purple pants, but some things are non-negotiable."

"We don't make anything in this house non-negotiable, Jen." Melanie said. "We prefer to talk out decisions with our kids and help them see the consequences of their actions. That way they can see the reasoning behind our decision-making process."

Ohhh Lord. Here we go, here we go! Good bye, fabulous listing!

I rolled my eyes. "You guys, there are *definitely* things that are non-negotiable. Does she have to sit in a booster seat in the car and wear a seat belt? Yes. Does she have to brush her teeth every day? Yes. Does she have to wear clothes when she leaves the house? Yes. She's *five*. There isn't much reasoning you can do with a five-year-old. Sometimes they just need to be *told* what to do."

"Simply telling a child to do something never works," Melanie said. "It must be her decision."

"Fine." I turned to Braxtyn. "Do you want to play outside today?"

"Yes."

"It's cold. Do you want to be cold the whole time you're out there?"

"Well ..."

"C'mon, Braxtyn. You don't. Just admit it. You'll be miserable and you won't have any fun at recess. You want to be warm and have fun, right?"

Braxtyn knew she was falling into a trap, but she wasn't sure how to stop. "Yes ..."

"Good. Now, go and put on your coat. *Please.*" I looked at Melanie and smiled. "Even though it's non-negotiable I still try to always make it a polite request."

We all watched in silence as their precious pumpkin Braxtyn walked slowly to the hook where her bright pink coat hung. She took it off the hook and pushed her arms through the puffy armholes. She zipped it up and stood there staring at us.

Melanie and Carl stared at me slack-jawed. Even Sanderson had stopped throwing oatmeal at me. *That* kid was a fucking nightmare, but I didn't have the time or the guts to tell them where to begin with him. Actually I knew where begin: saying "Uh-oh" repeatedly is never going to make him stop throwing oatmeal at people. That is not a consequence! The only consequence with that is that I finally go deaf from your repetitive "uh-ohs" and I go blind from the hot oatmeal searing my eyeballs.

However, I was already treading on thin ice with this listing and if I told Sanderson to knock it off, I would surely be fired—assuming I wasn't already.

I held my breath and waited for Melanie and Carl to fire me.

I'd clearly over-stepped my boundaries as a Realtor. I should not have lectured Carl and Melanie like I did and I certainly shouldn't have told Braxtyn to put on her coat. But as I sat there wiping globs of oatmeal off of my paperwork and kicking the dog off my leg, I decided I didn't give a damn if they fired me.

Fuck it, I thought.

So what if I lost the listing? It would be worth it. There is nothing worse than seeing a couple of passive parents let a preschooler walk all over them.

I'm just so tired of listening to parents cajole and negotiate with their kids to do things that should be expected. You shouldn't beg your kid to wear his coat on a cold day. You shouldn't ask your child to pretty please with a cherry on top buckle up her seat belt. No, no, no, no!

This is not a discussion amongst world leaders where everyone gets a say and we make compromises to prevent World War III. I'm your mother and we're not having a discussion. This is a hostile take over. There are no compromises for certain things. You must wear your damn coat. You must buckle your seat belt. You must do your homework. You must be respectful. You must eat your veggies. I could go on and on with the list I have for my kids.

Listen, don't think for a moment that I'm saying that my kids do this stuff willingly. Of course they don't! What kid willingly says, "Please pass the beets, mommy dearest?" NONE! It's our job to parent our kids. It's our job to make sure that they eat their beets or wear their coat. Sure, it's a battle sometimes, but I'm older and wiser and I'll die on that hill. My kids can't outlast me when it comes to this kind of stuff.

And here's the dirty secret: it starts out when they're five and it's a battle over coats, but before you know it, they're tweens and teens and you're battling over much bigger things. Like the passwords to their social media accounts. You're demanding to know what they're doing online and they're telling you it's none of your business, they can handle the consequences of their actions just like you taught them. Oh, really? So when your fourteen-year-old daughter sends a topless photo to an upper classman she's fully prepared for the entire football team to see that picture of her boobs? Or your son is that eighteen-year-old senior who is suddenly a sex offender because he was the douchebag who asked to see a fourteen-year-old's boobs?

And you don't know any of this until the cops show up at your house, because everything is a discussion and the kids get a say and a vote on matters that they never should have. This isn't "What do you want for dinner?" These are big issues and we have to protect our kids. Whether it's from the cold or from making a terrible decision that will affect the rest of his or her life.

The silence was broken when Carl cleared his throat and said, "Thanks for coming over, Jen. I'm sorry it was so chaotic. We'll do better next time." I quickly gathered up my things and Melanie walked me to the front door. *I guess I'm not getting fired,* I thought.

I stepped out into the bone-chilling wind. *Hell yeah, that kid needs a coat!*

I felt invincible, so I called back, "And tell Braxtyn she needs a hat too!"

CHAPTER 4

WELCOME TO NEW YORK, BITCHES

IN 1997, I arrived in New York City with only a suitcase and a dream! Oh wait, that's not true. Not even remotely. I arrived in my mom's old (but new to me) Jeep Cherokee full of snazzy Benetton sweaters mixed in with a couple of brand new power suits plus a fancy schmancy carry on rolly suitcase thing.

After six months of answering want ads in *The New York Times* and faxing countless resumes into black holes, I had finally received a legitimate job offer. I had managed to escape the drudgery of my job in a windowless basement at an engineering firm so that I could be engulfed in the monotony of professional conference planning for scintillating industries like Casualty Insurance and Asset Management. I didn't care how boring it sounded. It wasn't a windowless basement or digging ditches. I could pay my rent and it was in New York City where I could be closer to my new boyfriend I found on the Internet (who in five short years would become the Hubs).

Now that I was going to be darting around the country and hobnobbing with middle management insurance folk, my parents decided I needed to look the part. They knew the duffle bag-style luggage (personalized with "Jenni") from Land's End I'd received as an eighth grade graduation present wasn't going to cut it anymore, so they'd upgraded me to a working girl Samsonite on wheels.

I was moving to New York, because the Hubs and I had been dating long distance for a year at that point and we'd decided that if this relationship was going to move forward, it was time for someone to move. Since I'd spent several years of my childhood on the East Coast and had always wanted to live in New York City as an adult, I was more willing to move there. Good thing, because he had *no* desire to move to Kansas City and you can only call a guy you only chat with on the Internet your "boyfriend" for so long before people start to think you're thisclose to becoming a crazy cat lady slash hoarder. Plus, we figured if things didn't work out between the two of us, it was easier to disappear into a city of 8.2 million people than a city of 460,000. So if we broke up, we'd never have to worry about running into one another at the mall. Also, he'll never admit it, but I don't think the Hubs was ready to move out of his parent's basement just yet. Why would he? He had a pretty sweet deal there: free rent and utilities, free home-made meals, free laundry service, and two roommates who were always around to listen to him and loan him money. Sure, he had to put up with the occasional—okay, daily— lecture on personal responsibility and at twenty-six years old he still had a curfew. No, really. His mom was certain we were doing the nasty if he was at my apartment past 10 o'clock. So she would page him if he was out too late. Despite all of these hassles, he felt the pluses far outweighed the minuses.

My mom offered to drive across country with me and

help me get settled into my new apartment before my job started the following week.

Before our trip we spent some time at our local AAA where we picked up a few maps so we'd know how to get from Kansas to New York, because, this was a time before everyone had a GPS in their car or on their phone and you actually had to be able to read a map to get anywhere. (You young people under thirty just have no idea what our lives were like before all of this technology. We thought Walk Men and DVD players were the most high tech things we'd ever see in our lifetime. I mean, you could *walk* and listen to your mixed tape clipped on your belt. Mind. Blown.) Mom and I thought we were so smart and so on top of it when we got our maps from AAA. We asked the helpful AAA lady for directions to my apartment in Forest Hills, Queens. Unfortunately, the AAA lady was not very familiar with Forest Hills and none of us could locate my apartment on her map. I was going to live on Queens Boulevard and the best the AAA lady could do was get us to the middle of Queens Boulevard. Being the dumbass that I am, I thought, *No problem. How big can Queens Boulevard be?* (I've since found out that Queens Boulevard is about seven miles long and can be twelve lanes across in some parts and stretches across the borough of Queens. So, y'know, kind of big.)

I figured we'd get to Queens Boulevard and then we'd just follow street numbers until we found my apartment building. I really didn't take into account how busy the street would be and how hard it would be to see the numbers. The other thing I forgot is that both my mother and I are directionally challenged.

We made it to the middle of Queens Boulevard, but couldn't make heads or tails from the numbers. We were caught in a tangle of cars, blaring horns, and a crush of humanity. Our senses were overloaded and instead of figuring out where we were, we both sort of shut down and got even more lost. And that's how at one point, we found ourselves traveling in the wrong direction on Queens Boulevard. It wasn't until I finally stopped at a red light and asked a large, hairy, sweaty Greek man standing on the corner which way to Forest Hills that I found out I was going the wrong way. "It is other way. I take you," he offered.

"Oh no!" my mother replied, quite alarmed. "It's fine. We'll find it. Thank you, though."

"No. It's okay. I show you. I get in back," he reached for the door. I wasn't too worried, because my doors are always locked and even if he got the door open, there was absolutely no room for this gentleman in the back seat of my car unless he was going to sit on my priceless R.E.M. CD collection and the *hell* I was going to let that happen.

"Sorry, we don't have room," I said.

"I just make little space. I fit." He kept struggling with the door.

"Oops, the light is green!" Drivers behind me were laying on their horns and yelling at me to "Get a fucking move on."

"Fuck you!" the sticky Greek yelled to the drivers behind me. "These women are lost. I am helping them!"

"No, buddy, fuck *you*!" a driver yelled.

"Yeah! Get the hell out of the way!" another driver called.

"Jenni ..." my mom whispered. "The light. It's going to turn. If you don't hurry, we're going to be stuck."

I looked up and saw the light had turned yellow and I still hadn't moved. I was going to get us killed if I didn't get through that intersection.

"Thank you for your help!" I yelled and hit the accelerator, leaving the guy behind.

After we got a block or so down the road, my mom said, "Okay, okay. That was helpful and a little scary all at the same time, yeah? Let's just find a place where we can make a U-turn and go back and find your apartment."

I found a place to turn around and started heading in the right direction, cursing the Hubs' name. Now, at this point, you're probably wondering where the hell was the Hubs and why didn't I ask him for help. Well, there were a couple of reasons.

First, the Hubs was out of town when I moved in. Real romantic, right? Here I was moving across the country so that we could finally be in the same city and he couldn't be bothered to be there to greet me and help me when I arrived? Nope. He thought it was more important to take that same week to drive his brother from New York to California for graduate school. He made this big deal that his brother needed his help driving. I don't believe that for a second. He and his brother can barely stand to spend an hour together and I'm supposed to believe they wanted to spend days crammed together in a little car? I wasn't buying it. I don't think his brother even asked for his help, I think the Hubs just wanted to drive across the country and see the sights like the largest ball of twine plus get out of helping me move in. Asshole.

Second, the Hubs didn't drive much and when he did drive, he had no idea what the names of streets were. Getting directions from him is like when my Uncle Carl who lives in a small town in western Kansas, gives directions. Uncle Carl says things like, "Go about three miles until you see the big windmill farm—not the little one, the big one—then turn southeast on the third gravel road and that should take you into town. Just stop the first person you see—if no one is out, there's always someone at the Methodist church—and tell them you're looking for Carl and Josie's place and they'll point you in the right direction. If you hit the feed lots you've gone too far. Just turn around and go back and start again."

These were the Hubs' helpful directions: "Go across that one bridge and then jog over a few blocks until you see Queens Boulevard. Or you could take that other road next to it. I can't remember what it's called. Remember, I showed you my elementary school? That's the road I'm talking about. You could take that one for awhile and then it turns and takes you in the wrong direction, so you'll need to move over before you pass the hospital my mom used to work at. Not the one she works at now. Then once you're on Queens Boulevard, you just take it until you see your building. You should recognize it. It's five stories high and all brick." (If you've ever been to Queens, then you will know that probably eighty percent of the apartment buildings are five stories high and all brick.)

Even if he was around, I knew to never count on him for directions. He was always giving me terrible directions and then blaming me when I couldn't find what I was looking for. It still drives me crazy. Little did I know at the time, but one of the dumbest fights I'd ever have with the Hubs would be early on in our marriage when we had to drive across country he yelled at me for getting us lost even though I had nothing to do with it. I knew soon it would be my turn to take the wheel, so I closed my eyes for a little nap. After a couple hours, I was shaken awake by an irate Hubs. "You made me miss my turn and we've been going on the wrong highway for an hour!" he yelled at me.

"What?" I asked, snapping awake. "What are you talking about?"

"I missed the entrance to the highway and now we're an hour out of our way," he fumed.

"And how is this *my* fault?" I asked. "I was asleep! I didn't tell you to take the wrong turn."

"I know you were asleep. That's *why* it's your fault. I needed you to help me."

Now I was pissed. "You had a fucking GPS, you idiot!"

"I couldn't hear her over the radio!"

Moron.

So it was a good thing he was out of town, because he would not have been any sort of help anyway. My mother and I were better off without him.

"There it is!" My mother pointed down the road to a five story brick building on the other side of the street.

"Are you sure?" I squinted trying to see the numbers over the front door.

"I'm positive. Because when we came to sign the lease on the apartment, I remember that there was a Bed, Bath & Beyond right here and I thought we could get your drapes there."

"Oh yeah. You're right," I said. "I'm going to need a rug too. Perfect." My mom and I might be directionally challenged, but we always know our way to the closest big box stores that take our coupons and credit cards.

"Should we shop first?" she asked.

"Definitely!" It had been at least seventy-two hours since we'd last shopped and I was getting a little twitchy. I needed a hit. Plus, who wants to unload a carload of boxes when they can go and buy new shit instead?

We did some serious damage. Not only did I get a new rug and drapes, I also picked up a few new things. Like a new bedspread, because now I needed a new super hip and cool New York City style bedspread. My sweet country rose covered comforter with the lace dust ruffle wasn't going to cut it in the big city. (I may not make my bed very often, but when I do, I like it to be beautiful.)

We took a detour through the vacuum cleaner aisle so my mom could try and convince me that even though my apartment was all hardwood floors, a vacuum cleaner would be a terrific investment for me. My mom has an unholy relationship with her vacuum cleaner. I think if my parents got divorced my mom would fight harder for visitation with her vacuum than visitation with her dog. "You can't imagine how dusty the tops of your cupboards can get. A vacuum can get all of that for you," she explained.

"Mom, I've never cared about how dusty the tops of my cupboards are. No one can see them."

"What about under your refrigerator? That vent in the front gets so clogged up."

"Mom, it's going to be okay."

"I should have given you my old one. It's the perfect size for such a little apartment. The cord is long enough you would only need to plug it in once and you could vacuum your whole place. I'll bring it the next time I visit."

"I don't want it, Mom."

"You'll be glad you have it. You'll see."

I let her take her time caressing the plastic handles while admiring the bag capacity and suck power of each model. When she was done I bought a broom.

Finally, it was time to go. We'd put off unpacking the car long enough.

We headed down the street toward my apartment building, only to realize it was on the other side of the road and we couldn't see any way to get to it. Medians, one way streets and No U-Turn signs separated us from our destination. We sat at a red light looking at the building, trying to figure out how to get there. I was contemplating pulling an illegal U-Turn when it finally dawned on me that I would need to go around the block and come at it from the other direction.

"How will we unload? Is there a parking lot?" my mother asked.

"No. Just street parking," I replied.

"Not even a garage?"

"No, Mom," I scoffed.

"Why are you moving here again?" she asked.

"Mom, you know why I'm moving. I can't stay in Kansas City any longer."

"I just don't get it. You have a beautiful house there with a two car garage. [I'd just bought my first house the year before and I'd left it behind with really crappy renters.] You had a good job and I am sure you could find another. [I'd recently been fired from the consulting firm I'd been working at—or "downsized" as I liked to say—and the job prospects I had were awfully bleak.] You have lots of friends—"

I had to cut her off there. I wasn't going to argue the merits of my home or my ability to find a new job, but this was simply a blatant lie. "I don't have any friends, Mom. Everyone I know is married and starting on kids. There is no one to hang out with. We all know *you* are my best friend. How pathetic is that? I'm a twenty-four-year-old woman who hangs out with her mom every weekend when she's not chatting online with her boyfriend who most people think is imaginary! I've got to restart my life, Mom. I need a new city."

"Well, I don't think it's that pathetic that we're best

friends," my mom said sadly. "I kind of like it. And I'll miss you. You're my best friend too, you know."

Now I felt bad. My mom *was* my best friend. I hung out with her all the time and talked to her on the phone when I wasn't hanging out with her. And now I was leaving her for some guy and she was actually helping me. She had helped me pack up my house in Kansas City, she was dealing with my obnoxious renters, she was going to help me set up my new apartment, and then she was going to leave me to start my new and (hopefully) exciting life, and then I would miss her. But I couldn't tell her that. I'm not touchy feely like that and she is, so she'd get all sentimental and try to bring up how much we've experienced together over the years. That would be awkward and weird—for me at least. Instead I snapped at her, "Listen, bestie, keep an eye out for a parking spot, will ya?"

We looked around and couldn't see an empty parking spot anywhere. I thought about the television and the stereo in the backseat of the car and wondered how far we'd have to haul that shit. Suddenly, a spot right in front of the building opened up. "Look! A spot," I yelled. Damn! I still had to get around the block and the chances of that spot still being there by the time I made it were slight.

My mom understood that. "Hurry up! I'll see you there!" she yelled as she flung herself from the car. She dodged cars, buses, and pedestrians as she ran across twelve lanes of traffic and stood in the empty spot waving cars away.

It took me several minutes to get around the block and when I arrived at the spot, my mother was having a heated discussion with a man in a car blocking the spot.

"There she is!" my mother yelled to him. "I told you my daughter was coming! Now move it!"

The man's car inched forward slowly, giving me barely enough to room to parallel park for the first time since I was tested on that skill at age sixteen.

I nailed the parking job and got out of the car to start unloading.

The man was still sitting there scowling at me. "You got here just in time, lady!" he threatened through his open car window. "I was just about to run your goddamn mother over with my car."

My mother and I laughed nervously, because surely he was being sarcastic, right?

"What the fuck are you two laughing at? It's not a joke. You don't stand in a parking spot, unless you *want* someone to run you over!"

My mom put her arm around me. "My daughter is moving in today and we needed the spot so she can unload her car."

"I don't care, lady. Just don't let me see you doing that again, or I *will* run you over next time. You two are some stupid, crazy bitches," he growled. "Welcome to New York, bitches!"

My mother stood there with her mouth hanging open. She didn't want me to move to New York City. She wanted me to be happy, but she was suspicious of the Hubs' intentions and she worried I was making a huge mistake by uprooting myself from my family and moving across the country for some guy I met on the Internet who lived in his parent's basement. She didn't like the idea of me living alone in a big city. She hated the thought of not being able to have dinner together once a week. She despised the fact that now I was a plane ride away instead of a fifteen-minute car ride. I could not have made the move alone. She could have sabotaged my move at any time, but instead she did insane and amazing things like risking her life (literally) by running across a busy street so she could find me a parking spot so my day wouldn't be any more difficult than it already was. She has always been there to help me achieve my dreams even if they aren't ones that she agrees with. She has always trusted me to do what I think is best for me and she's stood by and helped me in any way she can, even if that means standing in an empty parking spot during rush hour in Queens and listening to some douchebag call her a bitch and threaten to run her over with his Impala, because that's what best friends do.

So, two stupid, crazy bitches stood there laughing and hugging each other in a cloud of exhaust and dust. And one of those stupid, crazy bitches bought the other a beautiful housewarming gift that night: a vacuum cleaner.

CHAPTER 5

THE HUBS CAN'T AFFORD ANAL SEX

DO you ever worry that your husband is cheating on you? I guess I do sometimes. Every now and again I wonder. Especially when he's late coming home from a meeting that should have taken an hour, tops. Or when he gets a random text in the middle of the night that he quickly deletes and tells me it was spam. That's when a little voice in my head starts whispering: "That's weird. Did he say he got lost coming home from dinner with his friend? We've lived in the same house for ten years!" or "Since when does spam come through text messages at midnight?"

I'll have these thoughts and doubt will start to creep in. *Maybe he is cheating on me,* I think. But then I take a closer look at the Hubs and I realize that no one else would put up with his shit. He wears the same clothes every day for several days until I nag him to retire that particular ensemble to the hamper. A girlfriend wouldn't put up with that nonsense. He's too cheap to buy me dinner without a coupon and I know that we use all of his "good" coupons. A girlfriend would demand a dinner nicer than what he can buy with the left over coupons. If she's lucky she could get a free chicken sandwich at Wendy's with a purchase and I don't think that would cut it for most girlfriends. He has recently stopped buying any sort of wax or gel to put in his hair. He's deemed these items frivolous and too expensive. His hair tends to grow straight out rather than down and so without product to tame his mane, he now closely resembles a Monchichi. A girlfriend would buy him wax and insist he use it.

Another reason why I know he isn't cheating is because he never leaves me alone! We work from home together, all day, every day. We spend every evening together. Weekends are family quality time. If he's sneaking out to meet a girlfriend, it isn't happening enough for me. It would be nice to be left alone sometimes. I beg him to go out with his friends and give me a night to myself in a quiet house where I can read or watch terrible TV without his commentary, but he will never do it. He leaves me home alone about three times a year. At most. If he does have a girlfriend whom he only sees three times a year, she's living the life.

No, I will convince myself, the Hubs isn't cheating on me. That guy is way too lazy and cheap to cheat on me. His wallet can't afford a girlfriend and his heart can't take that much sex. No matter what he thinks!

However.

The other morning we were changing the sheets on our bed. As the Hubs snapped open a fresh clean fitted sheet he casually asked, "Hey Jen, have we ever had butt sex?"

"What?" I sputtered, dropping my corner of the sheet.

"Butt sex." He studied my quizzical face and decided I must be stupid. "You know what I'm talking about, right?"

"You mean sex—in the butt," I clarified.

"Yeah, that." The Hubs dropped his corner of the mattress and looked at me. "Have we ever done that?"

At that point I was utterly speechless.

And then I had a few questions.

First, I realize that the Hubs wasn't pure as the driven snow when we met, but he also wasn't a man-whore. He didn't have that many partners! As far as I know butt sex is sort of a rare occasion. The White Whale of sex. Surely he would remember all of the people he's ever had butt sex with. The list can't be that long!

Second, I've been his wife for thirteen years and we dated for several years prior to that. Supposedly we've been in a loving and monogamous relationship during these fifteen-plus years, could he really not remember if he'd ever stuck his peen up my pooper?

I really didn't want to have this conversation with him, so I deflected. Much the way I deflect the kids when they ask me a question that I'm uncomfortable talking about. "Mom, why did the Tooth Fairy forget to take my tooth for the third time this week?" I like to ask questions when I'm avoiding answering a question. "Why do you think she forgot? Maybe you were naughty and ate too much candy and that tooth is rotten? Maybe she doesn't want rotten teeth? Or maybe she's been exhausted these last three nights and she can't be everywhere at once? Have you ever thought about her needs? Huh? Huh?"

I deflected the Hubs. "Have you *ever* had butt sex?" I asked him.

"Hmm," the Hubs thought for a few seconds before he answered. "No."

His response time was a bit slower than I would have preferred. There are several questions that I could answer with an emphatic and definitive "no" without any hesitation.

Questions like:

Have you ever tried crack?

Were you a man previously?

Have you ever killed anyone?

Do you like mayonnaise?

I would add to this list:

Have you ever had butt sex?

Why did it take him so long to answer? Why couldn't he remember?

"Are you sure?" I asked.

"About what?" he asked.

"About having butt sex. Are you sure you've never had butt sex?"

"Oh. Yeah, I'm sure."

"So, if you've never had butt sex then why would you ask me if we've ever done that?"

"I don't know. I couldn't remember for a second."

"Bullshit." I threw a pillow at him.

"Hey! What was that for?"

"Because you're an ass. You ask me if we've ever had butt sex because you can't remember, but then you said you've never done it. You're getting tripped up in your lies. What is going on?"

"Nothing," he said. "I couldn't remember. That's all."

I was furious. "What the fuck, dude? We've been together for over fifteen years and you can't remember what we've done together sexually."

"I get confused sometimes. I wasn't sure if it was real or a fantasy. That's all."

"You fantasize about butt sex?" I asked.

"Yeah," he shrugged. "Don't you?"

God no! My girlfriends and I will talk about a lot of things. We talk about our cycles, our hemorrhoids, our dry vaginas, our saggy boobs, but we don't talk about butt sex. I have no idea which of my friends have done that particular deed. It is not something we speak of. However, there is a suburban legend that makes the rounds every few years about butt sex.

The legend goes something like this: There's a certain part of town where the trophy wives live. They're the ones who keep the personal trainers and plastic surgeons in business. Every so often you'll see one of these ladies out and about with a certain purse. It's a purse that sells for $5,000. Since I'm the type of girl who doesn't have the looks to be a trophy wife and I shop for purses at the Coach Outlet store, I didn't really notice these purses. Then one night I was out for Mexican with a friend and we saw a trophy wife and this particular luxury bag go by our table.

"Hey, see that bag," my friend said.

"Yes."

"It's five grand."

"Wow. That's a lot."

"Yeah," she said, slurping her margarita. "You know how you get one?"

"What do you mean? They give them away?" I asked, digging into the queso.

"No. You've got to *earn* a bag like that."

I was confused. "How do you earn a purse?"

"You gotta take it in the ass," she said, wagging a tortilla chip at me.

I choked on my burrito. "You mean ... *anal?*" I whispered.

"Yup. That purse is the brown eye poke prize." She motioned to our waiter and asked for two more margaritas.

I waited until he was out of earshot, because I'm a fucking lady and then I said, "So let me get this straight. You take it in the shitter and you get to name your prize and they all pick that ugly ass bag?"

"Yeah. Nuts, right?"

"Why?"

"Because it's crazy expensive. They all get bracelets for push presents when they squeeze out the heir and the spare, but that's nothing compared to taking up the poop chute. That act is worth a lot more than some shit from Pandora. Y'know?"

"Wow. I wonder if it's like a secret society. You see someone with that bag and you know that they've been cornholed," I said. "I wonder what you get for the second time you take it in the back door?"

"I think maybe a Lexus," my friend said.

"Hmm," I told her. "Screw that purse. I don't want that thing. If I let the Hubs diddle my butt, I'm going straight for the Lexus."

The waiter set down two fresh margaritas and we toasted one another.

"No shit," my friend said, taking a swig.

I thought of this suburban legend as the Hubs and I made our marital bed together.

"If we had butt sex you'd remember," I told him.

"Why?" he asked.

"Because I'd be driving a Lexus."

CHAPTER 6

RAISING TINY THROAT PUNCHERS

IF YOU'VE READ EVEN a small portion of what I've written over the years, you will know that I can't stand mouthy, asshole kids. You will also know that many times when I rail against these little beasts, I am quick to point out that my children are NOT perfect. I just want their parents to acknowledge that their children are twats and to apologize for their behavior.

In the spirit of owning your own parenting fails, this is me apologizing for raising tiny throat punchers.

It was summer break and my kids were attending camp in the morning with several of their classmates. One morning I received a text message from Vivianna, the mother of their friends, Seamus and Philippa. Vivianna asked if Gomer, aged nine, and Adolpha, aged seven, could come over the next afternoon after camp to play with her kids.

Now, I rarely refuse a playdate that's not at my house, so I, of course, wrote back: HELL YES! Then she made it even better when she offered to pick them up from camp and take them to lunch as well. UR THE BEST! was my hastily thumbed reply.

The next afternoon I enjoyed blissful silence around my house.

When she dropped them off later that afternoon, Vivianna walked the kids to the front door and rang the bell. I answered the door and did the usual spiel: "Did you have fun?," "What do you say to Miss Vivianna?," etc. and then I turned my attention to my new best friend, Vivianna. "Hey, thank you so much, Vivianna. This was fabulous. Were they good? Any problems?"

Vivianna got a huge grin on her face and said, "Step outside, I have to tell you what happened."

We stepped out on the porch. "Is everything okay?" I asked, getting worried.

"So I told the kids that I'd take them out to lunch."

"Yes, thank you for that. Do I owe you some money?"

"Don't worry about it, Jen." Vivianna waved her hand. "Just listen. So, I let Seamus choose where we'd eat. He said, 'How about Chik-fil-A?'"

"Uh huh."

"Well, as soon as he said Chik-fil-A, your kids stopped talking. Like they went completely silent. So I asked them, 'Is that okay with you, Gomer and Adolpha?' I thought maybe they were allergic to chicken or something."

Uh-oh. I knew where this was going. In our house we have very strong feelings about businesses that don't support our liberal agenda. "What did they say?" I asked, fearful of the answer.

"Gomer said, 'It's just that our mom doesn't let us eat Chik-fil-A. She says that they don't support marriage equality.' And I was like, 'Whaaaat?'"

"That's true. I did say that," I said.

"Gomer told me he had to stop eating there because you didn't want to give them any more money to support causes you don't believe in. Is that true too?"

I shifted uncomfortably. "We try to let our position be known by voting with our dollars," I explained.

"Right. Wow. I had no idea you were so liberal, Jen!" said Vivianna. "I mean, I support stuff too, but I'm not going to give up delicious chicken."

"It can be hard sometimes, but I'm determined," I said.

"Anyway, I was like 'Oh, that's interesting, Gomer' because my kids don't even know about marriage equality let alone what businesses support it—or don't support it."

"I hope Gomer wasn't rude about it," I said. "We try to keep that sort of stuff friendly." I left off the "in front of the kids" part of that statement, because in private we rail against the hate-chicken-eaters.

"No, he wasn't at all. In fact he said, 'However, I wouldn't tell you no if that's where you wanted to take us for lunch, because that would be rude of me.'"

I sighed. "Oh good."

"But then he said, 'Also, I love the food at Chik-fil-A and I miss it. My mom would let me go if that's the only option I had.'"

"Oh poor Gomer!" I said. "He's just like his mommy. I crave that damn chicken more than anything else!"

"So, at this point, I think it's settled and I say, 'Great! So, we'll go there!' But then, Adolpha pipes up. She says, 'I don't care about Chik-fil-A and why we can't eat there anymore. I just don't like it and I don't want to have lunch there.'"

I'd forgotten about Adolpha. She's more Hubs than me and sometimes her filter doesn't always work. And she abhors Chik-fil-A. "Ohhh no."

"Right? So then Philippa says, 'How about this? How

about the boys get Chik-fil-A and the girls get McDonald's?' At this point, I'm exhausted and I'm ready to make everyone PB&J but I can't remember if your kids have a peanut allergy or not. So I'm like, 'Yes! How about that, Adolpha? Can you eat McDonalds or does your mom forbid that too?'"

I nodded. We haven't boycotted McDonald's yet. I can give up chicken, but I am completely addicted to McDonald's Coke and they're just too damn convenient. I can over-look their egregiousness every time an under-paid worker hands me a delicious icy Coca-Cola. I'm only human! I'm not a saint, damn it!

"Did she say she can eat there?" I asked.

"It's better than that! Adolpha says 'McDonald's chicken nuggets are made from pink slime.' Can you believe that? How does she know that?" Vivianna laughed.

"Oh. Yeah. That. Well, we watched a video on Youtube that was pretty disgusting about how the nuggets are made. I've quit eating them, but I can't quit the Coke."

"Do you show your kids how the chickens are slaugh-tered too?" Vivianna asked.

"No. I do have some boundaries, I guess," I said, shrugging.

"So back to my story. Now that Adolpha has told me about the pink slime, I'm like, 'Is that a problem for you?'"

"What did she say?"

"She said, 'Nope! I looooove pink slime nuggets!'" Vivanna shook her head, laughing.

"Classic Adolpha. She has no fucks to give."

"Exactly. So, I drive through Chik-fil-A and get the boys lunch and then I drive through MCD's and I get the girls lunch. We take it home and we have a great time."

I feel like this isn't the end of her story though. "And then ...?" I asked.

"And then about an hour after lunch, the girls come to me telling me they're bored. They tell me they want do something crafty. So, I decide I'll take them to—"

I cut her off. "Oh no, you went to Hobby Lobby didn't you?" I asked. Hobby Lobby is also on our boycott list. That one isn't too hard, because luckily they don't sell Coke.

"Yeah." Vivianna nodded.

"What did they say?"

"Your kids practically staged a sit-in! They refused to budge. They put up a unified front and they both told me that until Hobby Lobby starts valuing their female employees' reproductive rights they're never setting foot in that store again. Can you believe that?"

Actually, I could.

I didn't know what to say. My kids weren't *technically* assholes, but they were awfully opinionated for grade schoolers. I could only imagine how I would feel if I had to drive around town with tiny NRA-loving tots in my backseat demanding to know why I'm not carrying a concealed weapon when it's totally my right as an American citizen. I wouldn't be thrilled and I bet Vivanna wasn't either.

"I'm sorry, Vivianna. I hope you weren't offended by their behavior," I said.

"Oh it's fine. I wasn't offended," said Vivianna. "I was simply surprised that they have such ... *passion* for their beliefs."

I thanked Vivianna again and went back in the house. I felt a bit chagrined. I know that we talk to our kids about mature subjects and I know that we probably listen to way too much NPR in the car, but I can't help it. I'm not a hippie or a tree-hugger. I use plastic bags and I drive a gas-guzzling minivan. I waste water and I use entirely too much electricity. I'm also not a right-wing fanatic. I support equal rights and gun control. I think corporations are not people and should never be deemed as such. I think education is important and health care should be available to everyone. And I will do whatever I can to keep those fucking old male politician hands off of my daughter's reproductive rights!

I am trying to raise educated citizens of the world who care more about justice and ending world hunger than Kim Kardashian's ass.

In the kitchen I found Gomer lambasting the Hubs for wasting water and Adolpha absolutely livid due to a news story she'd overheard regarding the wage gap between female and male CEO's salaries. Between the eco-terrorism they learn at school and the feminazi propaganda I constantly spout, I realized I was raising a couple of passionate tiny throat punchers.

And I couldn't be happier.

CHAPTER 7

HEY DICK, WOULD YOU SEND YOUR MOM THAT PICTURE?

I'VE RECENTLY OPENED up my Facebook profile to allow anyone to friend me. I thought it would be a great way to connect with readers and get to know them better. At the beginning it was working perfectly. I got to engage one on one with my readers and see pictures of their favorite meals (mostly wine from what I can tell) and learn about their pet peeves (it's a lot of the usual assholes: kids, husbands, and pets.) I've enjoyed getting to know many of them better and actually becoming "friends."

Every morning I have new messages in my inbox and I'm always excited to see what's waiting for me. I am a mail whore. Not to be confused with a *male* whore. That's a whole other kind of whore! I am a whore for mail. I love mail. Always have. When I was a kid I would rush to the mailbox every day after school to see if I had a letter waiting for me. A card from the grandparents always ensured I'd be a few dollars richer. A letter from a friend from summer camp was typically full of juicy gossip. In those days I subscribed to nearly fifty billion magazines, so if nothing else I always had a new magazine or a subscription renewal notice.

When e-mail came into existence it was the greatest thing ever for me, because now I get instant gratification the moment I open my computer. Sure, it might be a coupon for Baby Gap waiting for me even though I no longer have children small enough to fit their togs, or a reminder from my kids' school that I owe more money on their lunch cards and if I don't hurry up and pay they will be cut off and forced to eat crackers and water, or a Nigerian prince who desperately needs my bank account info because he wants me to be rich, rich, rich! It might not seem like much, but it doesn't matter to me. It's mail!

With all of these new friends on Facebook now, my inbox never fails to disappoint. Most days I've got an e-mail or two waiting for me. A few of my new friends have reached out to tell me that they enjoy my writing. Why, thank you! I much prefer those e-mails to the ones who tell me they hate my writing. Those people kind of suck and I really wish they hadn't written. Actually, that's not true. Hate mail is still mail! A few new friends have asked me for advice or help with their writing goals. I like hearing from those people too. I always try to help my fellow writer types whenever I can. Some even invite me out for a drink and although I'm a little leery they might roll me for my sweet ass minivan, nothing gets between me and a free drink, so I throw caution to the wind, grab my pepper spray, and I go!

So what I'm trying to say is that I like mail. A. LOT. I never thought there would be a kind of mail I didn't like.

I was wrong.

You see, recently I received some mail I didn't care for. I received what is commonly referred to as: "a dick pic."

For those of you have never been lucky enough to

receive such a thing, let me explain. You get a private message from a "friend" on Facebook and when you open it up you are staring at a wrinkly one-eyed snake (assuming it's flaccid) or you are staring at a bulgy, veiny hot dog without a bun. After you scream a little and laugh a lot (because penises in any state of erection are both freaky and funny looking), you scroll down and you see a message from the dude who *supposedly* owns the baby-arm-size appendage pictured above. (Seriously. Why is it that dick pics are never average-size schlongs or tiny twigs and berries? Why are they always more Excalibur and less X-Acto?)

Hi Lovely,

I was thinking about you.
And this happened.
Want to see more?
LMK [That's douchebag-speak for "Let Me Know."]

XoXo

I have to admit, I was a little flattered that I had reached such a level of pseudo-wannabe-celebrity that I got a dick pic. I've always thought they were only for the popular girls and more than once I've had a twinge of jealousy that no one thought enough of me to send me closeups of their cum gun.

After I got over my initial feelings of flattery, I quickly moved into a feeling of utter and complete confusion. Now that I had this picture, what was I supposed to do with it?

Frame it and hang it on my wall? You know how people frame the first dollar they ever made? Are you supposed to do that with your first dick pic? I could take it to Michael's and ask them to frame it for me. I have a coupon. I could see how the conversation would go with the teenage helper behind the counter:

"Hi, may I help you?"

"Yes, please! I would like to get this framed."

"Um, ma'am, is that what I think it is?"

"If you think it's a chub, then yes, it's exactly what you think it is. You see, it's my first dick pic. This picture says that I have arrived!"

"I need to call my manager. We can't frame that here."

"Why not? I have a coupon for half off. It doesn't say anywhere in the small print that the picture I'm having framed can't be a man's erect and naked meat popsicle."

"Ma'am! This conversation is incredibly inappropriate. I'm going to have to ask you to leave."

"Wait. Are you telling me you won't frame this picture just because it's a skin flute? I was going to ask if you knew where I could have a little plaque made for it that says Jen's First Dick Pic."

"Please leave before I call the police!"

"Wow, I expected better from you guys. It's not like this is Hobby Lobby. Those ladies in the Hobby Lobby framing department have probably never seen a trouser trout before, but I thought you Michael's employees get around more. I thought you were the slutty craft store. I guess I was wrong."

At this point I'd probably be escorted from the store by security and asked to never return again.

Okay, so maybe I wouldn't frame it.

Maybe I should share it? Surely Dick—I thought it

might be appropriate to call the sender Dick from here on since that's the only part of his body that I've seen—maybe Dick wants the world to see his thunder sword. I could easily share Dick's picture and make his throbbing dong a superstar. I'm thinking of all those girls sitting at home pining for their own drum stick pic. I could share mine with them and make them feel just as special as I did when I first laid eyes on that fleshy meat stick. "You picked me! You picked me!"

Forget sending it in private messages, I could unleash it on the world. If I did that I could get in a lot of trouble though. I might be reported for spreading porn or something like that. All I was trying to do was make Dick's dick famous. Sheesh.

Okay, so maybe I wouldn't share it.

Maybe I was supposed to respond to him? It was technically an e-mail and I try to reply to everyone who writes me. What should I say?

I could go the friendly and polite route:

Dear Dick,

Thank you for the selfie. Or is it a dickie? Either way, your photo was a complete surprise. Thank you for thinking of me and becoming erect. When I make a list of life goals, "Make a stranger hard" is always on there and now, thanks to you, I can cross that one off the list. I can only hope that this is the first of many that you'll send to me.

Sincerely yours,
Jen

Or I could go to the sarcastic route:

Dear Dick,

I must say, wow. Thank you so much. Penises are my favorite.

I'm always interested in men who send dick pics. I mean, after all, that's what women are totally attracted to. We sit around all day analyzing who we think has a hot peter and who doesn't. Men like George Clooney sell millions of magazines, not because their faces are so handsome, but because we're all wondering, "Nice face, but what does his Ramburglar look like?"

It's like you understand women so well. You've really got us figured out. You know exactly what we like. It's not a strong jawline, or a luxurious head of hair, or a great sense of humor, or even a big bank account. We are all about the pork sword.

You must be a man of the world. A man who has to fight off the ladies with a (meat) stick. I highly doubt that you're an awkward middle-aged man sitting in your mom's basement wearing nothing but a pair of dirty boxers typing furiously on a Cheetos-dust-covered keyboard. I don't think for a moment that you searched online for "big penis" and then copied and pasted the first picture you found into an e-mail for me and thirty-five other women you thought enough of to troll on Facebook late last night. I'm positive that you got out your very expensive camera and truly thought about my old fluffy body and my graying lady garden and immediately felt the stirrings in your manhood (I mean, who doesn't, right?). I am sure that as soon as your love wand was ready for magic, you quickly snapped a picture of it and sent it to me like a modern-day love poem. If Lord Byron were still alive today, you know dick pics would be his preferred medium. Because nothing says, "Hey lady, I think you're smart and attractive and you've got your shit together. We should hang out and do great things together both in the sack and out of the sack" like a picture of your pecker.

I truly hope you keep the pictures coming. I can't wait to see more of them, because I am sitting here with bated breath wondering how many different angles you have of your longfellow that you can share with me.

In the meantime, I will be as patient as I can and keep myself content with the single snap I have. I will study your specimen and I will keep myself occupied wondering, "It looks good, but how does it taste?"

Best,
Jen

Or I could be just straight up honest:

Dear Dick,

WTF is your problem, dude? What in the world possessed you to send me a picture of your junk? Does your mother know you're using her Internet to accost unsuspecting women like this? Does that usually work for you? Do you get women to respond to you? Because I looked at it and I laughed my ass off. Penises are hilarious looking. Plus, the

*picture you sent me is clearly a professional taco warmer.
There is no way in hell you've got twelve inches in your
drawers and you're spending your Saturday nights sending
out pictures of your Tallywacker to strangers. If you had that
kind of game in your shorts, you'd be showing the goods to
real live ladies, not old ladies like me on Facebook.*

*You need to knock this shit off. No one wants to see your
penis (or some penis you found on Google). No one thinks
that's hot. It's the virtual equivalent of slapping a woman
across the face with your woody. That's just creepy, man. Is
that what you want? Do you want to be known as Dick the
Creeper? The guy who sends ladies unwanted pictures of
(other men's) pickles? If you really want to meet a lady, then
you need to shower and leave your mom's basement. You
need to find a woman who you find attractive and speak to
her face and never once show her a picture of your penis. Be
a fucking man, not a fucking creeper.*

*Maybe if you actually behave normally and meet a woman
who likes you, she'll ask to see your vagina miner. That is the
goal here, right? To get laid?*

*Now, if you ever send me a picture of your peen again, I
promise you, I'll put your Tiny Tim on my blog along with
your email address and ask the world to flood you with
pictures of assholes. Like actual hairy assholes, you asshole.*

Got it? Good.

See you around,
Jen

CHAPTER 8

LAURA INGALLS WILDER NEVER HAD A SIGNATURE LIP SMACKERS FLAVOR

I DON'T KNOW about you, but I've always been a little behind my peers and socially awkward. My friends were always way more experienced than I was and I just sort of played along like I knew what they were talking about, when really I was completely in the dark most of the time. It became very apparent just how far behind I was when I hit fifth grade.

While it seemed like everyone else around me was moving on and experimenting a bit with boys, I was still watching *Little House on the Prairie* and collecting stickers and stuffed animals. The only thing I was more advanced in than anyone else was my swear word vocabulary. They all knew how to French kiss, but I had perfected the fine art of telling someone to fuck off. I didn't learn how to swear from watching *Little House.* Riding the bus taught me how to properly conjugate "fuck." As in, "You guys, I fucking loved *Little House on the Prairie* last night. It was awesome when Laura pushed Nellie down the hill in her wheel chair. Classic."

It was the end of the school year when I was invited to a pool party at a pseudo-friend's house. The girl hosting the party, Megan, wasn't really my friend. She was a friend of a friend and because this was fifth grade, her mother had obviously made her include me on the guest list in the event I might possibly hear about it through the grapevine and get my feelings hurt.

By this point I already had body issues and a pool party would surely not be my first choice when it came to socializing. I would have preferred we wait until winter and have a sledding party where everyone could waddle around in snow pants. However, I liked a lot of the people going and I wanted to try and fit in more with the cool girls like Megan. So I squeezed into a swimsuit and headed over.

I should mention here that I wasn't a chunky monkey yet. Not even close. When I look at pictures of myself from that time I'm shocked. I remember feeling like a whale. I remember thinking my legs were like blubber and my tummy like jelly. However, when I look at pictures from that time, I want to go back and smack myself up the head. Sure, the girl in the pictures is definitely a bit thicker than everyone else. She's compact and muscular and she's softly rounded already while the rest of her friends are still rail thin with long gangly limbs, but at 41 I would kill to be this "fat" again. *Puhleese.* I'll take those blubbery legs and jelly tummy now.

I threw a t-shirt over my swim suit, because compared to the other girls in my class, I already had quite a bit of boobage at that point, so I preferred to wear a t-shirt over my swim suit when I went swimming. Like an idiot, I was under the false impression that this hid my contours and shielded prying eyes. It wasn't until later in life that I learned about wet t-shirt contests. I never said I was the brightest bulb.

Megan lived in what I considered to be a mansion. It was a huge old house surrounded by several acres of gently rolling hills. When I arrived at the door, a maid (House-keeper? Domestic? Nanny? I don't know the appropriate word here. "Maid" makes it sound like I'm going to a pool party at *Downton Abbey*, but I don't know what else to call her. All I know is Megan was rich and cared for mostly by people on the payroll. Her parents were always off playing tennis or golf at "the club" or vacationing somewhere.) Anyway, the uniformed lady who was in Megan's parent's employ shooed me out the back door of the manse and told me to follow a flagstone path over the hill where I'd find the pool party.

As I got closer I could hear a boom box blaring Joan Jett and high pitched squeals of laughter followed by loud splashes. *Great,* I thought. *The boys are pushing the girls into the pool.* I pulled my t-shirt tighter around my body. *Nobody had better touch me or I'll fuck them up,* I thought. I think it's important to note here that although I tend to have violent ideas, I've actually never been in a fight in my life. I wouldn't even know how to begin to "fuck someone up," but it makes me feel better to think I have that option available to me.

Earlier that year the boys in my class had discovered that I was one of the few girls in the class who wore a bra and they took enormous delight in snapping the strap across my back. I despised it. It was humiliating to have the entire class laugh at me because some fucking moron thought it was funny to snatch at my bra. My swim suit did not have a strap across the back, but I didn't want any boy even getting close enough to figure that out. *No touching. No touching. No fucking touching!* I repeated to myself like a mantra.

When I got to the top of the hill, some of the kids saw me. "Hey, Jenni!" yelled my friend Michelle. "Hurry up! We need help. The boys are throwing us in the pool!"

Ugh. What would Laura Ingalls do? I wondered. *She'd be fishing with her Pa and never be at this party! Why did I come?*

Instead of joining the fray, I settled into a shady spot next to a girl named Shayla and watched the flirting around me commence. "Oh my God, Jenni, look at Brandon's butt. Isn't it so cute?" Shayla asked.

I looked at Brandon's butt. I could barely make out a bit of a bump that was slightly butt-shaped in his ridiculously large Jams. "So cute," I agreed. *What the hell was I talking about? I couldn't even see his ass, let alone make an intelligent assessment of whether or not it was cute. Would Laura Ingalls check out her classmate's ass? I don't think so!*

"Don't you think he's hot?" Shayla asked.

"Who? Brandon?" I asked.

"Of course, Brandon! He's so hot, right?"

"Umm ..." I hesitated. I was not comfortable with boys the way many of my friends were. Sure, I thought some boys were cute, but I was way too shy to tell them I thought they were cute, and even if I got up the nerve, I didn't know what to do beyond that. Michelle talked a lot about making out. I wasn't sure exactly what this meant. I was an avid reader and some of my books described making out as something as simple as a kiss and others talked about "bases." That just confused the hell out of me. What the hell did baseball have to do with making out? I was pretty sure they were related somehow, but I just wasn't sure *how*. So I said, "Yeah, I bet he's totally good at baseball."

"What? He plays football," Shayla said.

"Yeah he does. When he's not doing the *bases* with girls," I said knowingly.

"Jenni, you totally need a clue!" Shayla said. "You have no idea what you're talking about!"

She was right. One day I was in the bathroom with Michelle and I asked her if she'd ever made out with anyone. "Of course, silly!" she replied while reapplying her watermelon flavored Lip Smacker lip gloss.

"That's why I wear watermelon Lip Smackers. *Mmmm*. The boys love the taste of this flavor!"

Wait. What? The boys lick your lips when you make out? That sounded disgusting. Thanks to that conversation, I had no desire to make out. Ever.

For my birthday that year Michelle gave me an assortment set of Lip Smackers and encouraged me to find my "signature" flavor. Even though Laura Ingalls would never have had a signature flavor, I decided I would try and get with the times and find mine. The strawberry was okay, the watermelon was too overwhelming (even my hair smelled like watermelon when I wore it), the grape and the banana were both disgusting. Then I tried lemon-lime. It tasted delicious and I couldn't stop reapplying. In one short afternoon I went through the entire tube, because I kept licking it off my lips. *Yum!* The only thing that stopped me was when my lips became unbearably chapped and I realized I was sort of making out with myself. I put the Lip Smackers away and never got them out again. My signature flavor became medicated ChapStick.

"David! You got my hair wet!" Megan yelled, splashing him back.

"Well, it *is* a pool party. Aren't you supposed to get wet?" asked David with a grin. David was the dream boat of the fifth grade: a bit androgynous with scrawny little arms and legs, a bright smile, and a great head of hair. I found him on Facebook a few years ago. He's still adorable. He's married now—to a guy. I'm not surprised, he was a great listener.

"Heh. Heh. You said 'get wet'," chortled John. John was the dumbass of the fifth grade. Big and stupid and a total jackhole. I've never looked him up on Facebook, but if I had to guess where he is now, I'd say he's the Used Car Salesman of the Year in some crappy little town, sporting a fierce comb over.

"Eww, you're so gross, John!" Megan laughed.

John wagged his eyebrows at her.

I didn't get it. What was gross about being wet? I watched them closely trying to puzzle out what the problem was exactly.

"You've got smoke coming out of your ears, Jenni," Michelle said, flopping down on the chaise beside me. "What are you thinking about so hard?"

"What John said. Why is it gross to be wet?"

"Haha! Hey you guys, Jenni doesn't know what John is talking about!"

Everyone stopped what they were doing to stare at me. John looked me up and down and leered, "I'll show her what I'm talking about."

"Oh shut up, John. No one wants you," Shayla said.

"That's not what your mom said last week, Shayla!" John called diving under water.

Shayla's mom hangs out with John? I thought, *That's kind of weird.*

"John!" cried Doreen jumping out of the pool. "John just pinched my butt!"

Everyone laughed some more.

I wanted to go home. I did not want to be there. I did not want John to show me why it was gross to be wet and I definitely did not want him to pinch my butt. If Laura Ingalls was there, she would have punched John in the nose and gone home already. The only reason why I didn't leave was because Megan's house was so damn far away. Ugh. Why did they have to build the pool a half a mile away from the house? It was hot and the last thing I wanted to do was walk all that way so I could call my mother to come and get me. Plus, my mom would be pissed because Megan didn't live close to us and she was probably just now getting back home to our house and she would never want to turn around drive back again to pick me up. Nope. I would just have to stick it out.

And then Tammy arrived. "Hi guys!" Tammy called, as she breezed in the gate. Every boy stopped and admired her as she peeled out of her swim suit cover up. She was wearing a two piece and she was filling it out nicely. Even *I* could see that. She was tall and tan and leggy and bosomy, but like good, firm bosomy, not floppy bosomy like me. She got out her watermelon flavored Lip Smacker and applied a healthy dose.

The boom box started blasting Olivia Newton-John's *Physical*. "How appropriate!" Tammy said. "Who wants to play Seven Minutes in Heaven?"

"You know I do!" John yelled, shaking off the pool water like the dog that he was.

"Well, then let's go! Megan, you keep track of the time."

The two of them headed into the pool house.

I'd never played this game before. "What are they doing in there?" I whispered to Michelle.

"Whatever they want," she whispered back.

"Like talking or something?"

"No stupid! No one talks during 7 Minutes in Heaven," Michelle scolded.

"Oh. Are they making out? Doing the bases?"

"I guess so. You never know with Tammy," Michelle said mysteriously.

"What do you mean? They're not having ... *sex*?"

"I don't think so. I don't think they could do it that fast. It's only seven minutes. I'm pretty sure sex takes like half an hour."

"How do you know it takes half an hour?" I asked.

"My neighbor, Kelly, who is an eighth grader had sex over Christmas break and she told me."

"Kelly's the pregnant one, right?"

"Yup."

"Well, I guess she'd know how long it takes."

"Yeah. My guess is they're probably just making out. Or giving BJs. Katie says I should just do those so I won't end up like her."

"BJs? Don't they play music?"

Michelle shook her head. "Jenni, I can't even believe how dumb you are sometimes," she said. "I can't keep explaining everything to you. Let's just assume they're making out in there."

"*Eww*. I can't believe Tammy is making out with John. He's so gross."

"Yeah, but he *is* the best kisser in the class."

"How do you know?"

"I spent seven minutes in a coat closet with him last weekend at Heather's sleepover. He and Daniel snuck in the basement window after her parents went to sleep. By the way Daniel is a *terrible* kisser. He's super sloppy. Avoid him at all costs. Anyway Heather has kissed just about every boy in the class including John and she said he's the best. Also, she said he's got good hands."

"I see." I shuddered at the thought of his meaty hands touching me.

"Who've you had that's any good?"

I didn't have the heart to tell her that I hadn't kissed one boy. So I shrugged my shoulders and said, "Eh, oh you know. So far no one, if you know what I mean." I winked at her.

"Oh I *do* know what you mean! Don't worry. You'll get a chance at John and then you'll have something to talk about."

"No way, I'm never kissing John. He's a fucking asshole "

"Jenni! You better watch your mouth. One of these days a mom or a teacher is going to hear you and you'll be in trouble."

"Oh I don't give a flying fuck who hears me say that John is a dickhead and if he comes near me I will fuck him up."

"I know he seems like a jerk, but that's only because he knows he's so good. He's really gentle though. He has soft lips."

"His lips remind me of a carp." I felt the bile rise in my throat just thinking about his big, slimy, fishy lips coming at me in the dark. Oh hell no!

"Time's up!" Megan yelled banging on the door of the pool house. "Give someone else a chance, will ya?"

John and Tammy emerged looking a tad bit tousled. John high-fived Eric, the boy closest to him.

Ugh.

"Who's next?" John yelled.

"All right, I *guess* I'll go," sighed Michelle with faux reluctance.

I resisted throwing up as the door to the pool house closed behind her and John.

David said, "This game kind of sucks."

Oh thank God! Finally, someone was going to speak up.

"We should play something else," he said.

"We could play Marco Polo," I suggested.

"You're really funny, Jenni," David said.

"I am?" *Hmm, I wasn't really trying to be. I think Marco Polo is a fun pool game.*

"What are you thinking, Dave?" Eric asked.

"You got a bottle anywhere, Megan?" David asked.

"You know I do. I always keep one down here at the pool," Megan answered.

A bottle? I wondered. *A bottle of what? Aspirin? Did David have a headache?*

Suddenly the pool house door burst open and Michelle came flying out looking pissed.

"You're such a jerk, John!" she yelled.

"What's the big deal?" John asked following her. "It was just a little over the shirt grab. No big whoop."

"Whatever, John," Michelle said.

"All right, you lovebirds, listen up," Tammy interrupted. "David wants to play Spin the Bottle."

Spin the Bottle. This one I knew. Well, I only knew it because I'd read about it. I'd never played it before.

"Let's go in the pool house," said Megan. "We don't want prying eyes."

I lingered outside the door as long as I could. "Come on, Jenni! We're starting!" Michelle called.

Shit! This was a big deal! Whoever that bottle landed on when I spun it was going to be my first kiss! This is not at all how I envisioned my first kiss, it was supposed to be sweet and romantic—and preferably when I was in high school! I had it all planned out. It was supposed to be on a starry summer evening on my front porch after the best date ever or maybe during a quiet walk through the woods gathering fall leaves with my perfectly adorable boyfriend. Either way it was supposed to be *private*. Not in front of ten kids from my class!

And then I had the worst thought: what if the bottle landed on John?! Oh God! I did not want *John* to be my first kiss! I wracked my brain, *What would Laura Ingalls do?* First of all, Half Pint would never be in this situation. She would have never come to this stupid party where she'd be in a situation where she might have to kiss Willie. She'd fake an illness or do something harebrained that would cause a lot of unnecessary drama, but get her out of the situation.

I was just about to fake a seizure when I heard, "Hey, Jenni, I saved you a spot by me." It was David and his beautiful smile.

A spot? Next to him? I was like a moth to flame. "Okay," I mumbled and followed him blindly to my place. I could fake the seizure later if necessary.

Tammy took the first spin and got Eric. "Open mouth or closed?" she asked.

Shit! There are choices? There is more than one way to kiss? I was fucked.

"Open," he said.

Tammy unhinged her jaw and Eric's face disappeared into her gaping maw. I'm pretty sure I gasped. I was glad to see that Michelle was also a bit uncomfortable with the show. John, the pig, licked his lips.

David reached over and took my hand. "My turn," he said giving my hand a squeeze before he went to the center of the circle for his spin. He got the girl next to me, Tracy. He gave her a light peck on the lips and then returned to his seat next to me. "Darn," he whispered. "Just one more spot was all I needed." *What? Was he talking about me or Shayla, the girl sitting on the* other *side of Tracy?*

I was lucky enough to dodge the bottle every time. Finally, Michelle noticed I hadn't had a turn.

"Hey Tammy, let Jenni take your spin. She hasn't had a chance yet."

"Oh no, it's okay. I like watching."

"Oh do you, Jenni? Seen anything you like?" John leered.

"Shut up, John," David said. "Jenni, go spin the bottle. See who you get. Good luck."

My stomach was in knots as I moved into the circle and took hold of the bottle. *I want to go home. I want to go home,* I chanted inside my head. I gave the bottle a half hearted spin hoping it would break or someone would suddenly yell, "I'm bored! Let's go play Marco Polo!"

The bottle landed on David. "Finally," he said grinning. He closed his eyes and waited.

I felt sick to my stomach. Don't get me wrong, David was cute and I think every girl in the circle wanted to kiss him when it was their turn, but this was my *first kiss.* Under different circumstances I might have allowed David to be that person, but not with everyone watching us. I was terrified. I had no idea what I was doing. What if I was super sloppy like Daniel? I couldn't have the whole class saying I was terrible kisser and to avoid me at all costs. What if he asked for open mouth? I couldn't do what Tammy did. I wasn't even sure my mouth could open that wide.

I felt everyone's eyes on me. Watching and waiting. I

was going to throw up! Oh God, what if I went to kiss David and I threw up on him instead?

It was time to fake a seizure. I was so petrified that I could only get one eye to twitch and my body barely convulsed. When I realized it wasn't going to happen, I bailed. "I gotta go," I said, jumping up from the circle and dashing towards the door.

"What the hell, Jenni?" Michelle said.

"What just happened?" David asked.

"You can't just leave in the middle like that!" John yelled. He swiped at me and accidentally got a handful of breast.

"You just grabbed my boob!" I screamed at him.

"Oh, whatever, prude." John shrugged. "It wasn't even that great!"

Everyone watched us and no one said anything. I was rooted to the ground. Seething. Forget my first kiss, that motherfucker would go down in history as the first boy to touch my boob! *Oh hell no!*

"I. Want. To. Go. Home."

"No one's up at the house. It's after four. Irene leaves at four," Megan said. "I'll take you up in a few minutes and you can call your mother. Why don't you sit down and get a hold of yourself? You're freaking out over nothing. John barely touched you. God, you're so embarrassing. I can't believe my mother made me invite you." She slammed the pool house door behind her.

I wrapped myself up in a towel and waited. After a little while Megan's mother arrived with a tray of drinks and snacks. "Well, hello, Jenni," she said. "Where is Meg and everyone else?"

I debated what to tell her. I could make up a lie and somehow warn everyone in the pool house that Megan's mother was here or I could do what Laura Ingalls would do and serve them up on a platter. At that point I was ruined anyway. There was no making it better, so I decided to go out in a blaze of glory.

I smiled sweetly and popped a chip in my mouth, "They're all in the pool house—having sex."

CHAPTER 9

MISSED MOM CONNECTIONS

ONE OF MY favorite creeper things to do is to read the Missed Connections section of the local newspaper and Craigslist. They are usually full of horny dudes who spotted a hot chick on the elliptical at the gym last week. They're typically something equally disgusting and intriguing like:

Monday, 6 AM, 24-Hour Fitness. You're the blonde chick wearing hot pink Lululemon yoga pants, no VPL, but plenty of camel toe. Yum! You were OWNING that elliptical machine. Your body was banging and I'm pretty sure you were checking me out too. I was the guy blazing on the rowing machine in the Under Armour shorts, no shirt, and killer abs (it's not bragging if it's true). I didn't see a ring, but I can't believe a prize like you is still on the market. If you want to grab a drink, babe, find me this week. I bench every morning at six.

I'm disgusted, because this guy sounds like a total douchenozzle, but I'm intrigued becauseI always wonder if the Lululemon lady responds to him. If she's like, "Oh my

God, what a catch! Just what I was hoping for!" Can you imagine telling people that's how you met? "Well, Nick was working out one morning and he just about blew his wad when he saw me walk in with my see-through Lululemons I was wearing without panties. He left me a Missed Connection complimenting me on my body and inviting me for a drink and the rest is history!"

Just when I think chivalry is dead and all men think about are camel toe and VPL, I'll find an example of a good guy:

Friday, 3 PM PetSmart. I was hanging out near the chew toys with a black and white Boston Terrier. I spotted you with a light brown Beagle and two kids. We made solid eye contact and then you told me that the chew toy I was looking at was a choking hazard for my dog. (Thank you, BTW. I'm a new dog dad and I still have a lot to learn obvs.) When I thanked you, you dazzled me with your smile. Wow. Your kids were really well-behaved. I didn't see a ring and I got the impression you're a single mom?? (Dare I hope?) I felt too nervous to talk to you in front of the kids, but I'd love to buy you (and your Beagle) lunch if you're interested.

I'm really rooting for those two (assuming she's available)!

These Missed Connections got me thinking. There should be a Missed Connection site for moms. How many times have you been at the park and you've seen a mom you think you could be friends with, but you lost the nerve to ask for her digits because she might think that's weird? How many times have you wanted to introduce yourself to a table full of laughing moms out to dinner together, but then you got sidetracked worrying that they might be laughing at you?

That's why I'd love to see Missed Connections for Moms. I can only imagine what those Missed Connections for Moms would look like:

Tuesday, 1 PM, Sunset Point Ridge Trail Elementary School Room Mother's Meeting. You were the only one besides me who wasn't taking notes about how to be the "best Room Mother ever." I was in the back live-Tweeting how bored out of my mind I was. Maybe you follow my hashtag? #PTAsux. Did we really need fifteen minutes to discuss the colors of the Teacher Appreciation cupcakes? Who cares if they're purple and green or green and purple and how are those different from one another?? You were crushing some serious Candy on your phone. The Vice President of Room Moms introduced you as a transfer from out of town. She was babbling so much I missed your name. Christy, maybe? She asked what your Room Mom expertise was at your old school and you replied, "Winging it." I was the only one who laughed. When the VP accused the teachers of stealing PTA-paid-for Post-It Notes, I was the one who snorted. As you can see, my expertise is "Pot stirring." I'm a Room Mom because I like the teachers better than the moms. I am lobbying to have next month's meeting at a bar. I'm hoping if I get a drink in some of those ladies, they might relax a bit. Either way, I'm sure I'll see you at the meeting. I'll save you a seat in the back where we can heckle the VP.

Monday, 10 PM, SuperTarget. We were both digging through the banana bin looking for anything that wasn't spoiled. You were wearing yoga pants and I had on fuzzy PJ pants with bunnies on them. You offered me a coupon for Stouffer's lasagna because you said you only serve homemade lasagna to your family. I snatched that coupon out of your hand before you could change your mind (because Stouffer's is not cheap) and I asked you where you found chai, because the shelf was empty when I looked. You confessed that you were the one who cleaned them out and you shared your stash with me. We had a connection at that point. I felt it. Even though your cart was full of organic quinoa and mine was full of frozen dinners, I saw your copy of *Bossypants* sticking out of your Coach outlet purse. You caught me eyeing the book and I saw you checking out my Coach outlet purse. I was just about to invite you for chai, but I got nervous and then we were interrupted when my husband called. I had to take the call because I'd ignored his twenty previous texts telling me that the baby had a blow out and he needed me home ASAP. If I ignored him any longer he was either going to call 911 or divorce me. By the time I got off the call, you were gone. I'm in the produce aisle of Super-Target every Monday night at 10 PM. It's my "me time," but I'm willing to make it "us time." Maybe I'll find you there next week. I'll bring the chai, you bring Tina.

⊏▭⊐

Wednesday, 4 PM, Ironsides Park—The Swings. Our kids were waiting patiently in line for their turn on the swings, but there was a total pain in the butt mom who wasn't making her kids share. We both rolled our eyes and stifled giggles when she told Esmerelda and Lux that as soon as they got home she was going to make them certificates for being the "Best Swingers at Ironsides Park." We both sighed heavily and tried to make it known that we weren't happy with Lux and Esmerelda's behavior or their mother's. She continued to search Pinterest on her cell phone. I assume for incredible birthday party ideas for Esmerelda. How many times did that kid tell us she was going to be five soon? (WTF, kid? We get it. You're having a birthday. Your mom is crafty and amaze-balls and you're going to have a spectacular party. Blah, blah, blah.) Anyway, you were the one glaring at Lux while I kept mouthing "I hate you" to Esmerelda. I heard you politely mention it might be time for Lux and Esmerelda to vacate the swings and let others have a chance. The mother looked at you like you said, "Get your fucking kids off the swings already." Don't worry. You didn't say it out loud. I knew that's what you were thinking though, because I was too. At that moment I knew we could be besties. I was the one who chimed in "Yeah!"

I'll be at the slide on Sunday afternoon. I hope Lux and Esmerelda aren't there, but if they are, I'll have your back when you push Lux down the slide like I know you want to.

———

Thursday, 9 AM, Kindermusik Class. You rolled in fifteen minutes late with egg in your hair and a toddler gnawing on an uncooked Pop-Tart. You said you were late because you got a speeding ticket. Someone tried to pick the egg out of your hair and you laughed at her and told her it was your "leave-in conditioner." I think you were joking, right? Your sweat pants were inside out because that was the "cleaner" side and you weren't wearing a bra, because you couldn't find one that morning. I had the toddler who stood by the door and screamed during the entire class. She only stopped when your son finished his Pop-Tart and bit her. I think she was stunned into silence. No one has ever treated her so poorly. She needed it though. I was the one crying in a corner because this motherhood thing is so damn hard! Believe it or not, I think you're a hotter mess than I am. Just being around you made me feel like a mom with my stuff together. Thank you for that.

Thursday, 9 AM Kindermusik Class. You were sobbing uncontrollably and your daughter was a freak show screaming her head off. I just want to say, Hey girl, it gets better. I'm not sure if you noticed, but I have motherhood by the horns! Don't sweat it, though. You don't make motherhood your bitch right out of the gate. It takes time. I'm on my fourth kid, so it's taken me years to get to this point. Sure, I was a little late that morning and my son was eating a Pop-Tart because he chose to throw the last egg in my hair, but we got there, damn it. I got him there because I'm a good mom. Wearing clean clothes and a bra doesn't make you a good mom, showing up does. And I showed up. I showed up and my kid had his motherfucking music class and it stimulated his tiny brain and increased his vocabulary, or whatever shit singing to him is supposed to do for him. I am sorry he bit your kid, I admit that was a bit of surprise. Even with four kids you might be shocked to know that I've never had a biter before, but honestly, she had it coming with all that screaming. I was ready to bite her myself. Hang in there and I'll see you next week, Momma!

CHAPTER 10

THE BIRTHDAY DINNER WHERE WE ALMOST DIED A HORRIBLE DEATH, BUT THE CHICKEN SPIEDINI WAS DELICIOUS

IT WAS the week of the Hubs' birthday. My parents took my family and my mother-in-law (who had just moved to Kansas from New York City) to dinner to celebrate. We knew there was severe weather coming, but this is Kansas. We can't cancel dinner every time there's a severe weather warning. That would be like Canadians canceling dinner plans because there's snow in the forecast. We're always under some sort of severe weather watch. Plus, the Hubs wasn't about to miss a free meal.

So, we threw caution to the (70 mph) wind and headed out to the restaurant. We were sitting in a noisy restaurant when my mother said, "Shhh. Listen. Are those the tornado sirens?"

I listened carefully. YUP. Those were definitely tornado sirens. We were near the back of the restaurant, so they sounded kind of weak, but I could hear them.

Now, being a child of the Midwest I have had tornado safety drilled into my head since the wee age of five when we were taught at school that when you hear tornado sirens that means: "Take shelter now! Death in the form of a swirling vortex of wind, mud, two-by-fours studded with rusty nails, tractor trailers, and cows is coming towards you and will be upon you in a mere matter of seconds. Grab your loved ones and nothing else! Run! Run! Run! I hope to see you on the other side of this terrible storm! God save us all!"

However, in the last few years, I've noticed that those-who-are-in-charge-of-the-sirens have been been blowing them more as: "Hey, this is mostly for C.Y.A. purposes. Our lawyers suggested we turn on this siren. I mean, it's looking *kind* of bad and it could get worse, but who knows? You should probably look out your window and decide what to do. You could seek shelter, you could turn on the news and see what the radar says, or you could just keep doing what you're doing. Either way, I'm covered, because I warned you. I think you should definitely not be outside right now, though, because it's getting nasty out, y'know? Hey, I know! Go to your basement and watch the weather report. Yeah. Do that. Okay? Good talk. I hope this doesn't end up being a serious storm. I guess we'll know in an hour or so."

So when I heard the sirens, I didn't immediately grab my children and head for the meat locker.

Yes, the meat locker. True story: many, many, many (oh so many!) years ago when I was a single lady I spent a scintillating Friday night in the meat locker of my local grocery store, because I was hungry and decided I needed food during a tornado watch. I actually didn't realize there was a tornado watch going on. But even if I did I'm not sure I would have done anything different, because as I said before tornado watches are commonplace around here and bitches gotta eat. As soon as I walked into the store, the manager said, "Why are you out? Don't you hear the sirens?

Don't you see the sky? It's green! Get to the back of the store! Now!"

I spent the next half hour huddled together in the meat locker with forty or so employees and shoppers. It was cold and uncomfortable, but we were assured we weren't going to die at least. I shivered in a corner while scoping out the group I was sequestered with. I was hoping there was a hunky fireman type who was also trapped in there who would immediately fall in love with me because of our shared near-death experience. What? I watched a lot of Lifetime back then. He'd find me plucky and self-assured in the face of certain death and naturally beautiful even though I hadn't showered all weekend and I was dressed a lot like a boy. Shut up. He could see my INNER beauty!! Needless to say, it would be the best story to tell our friends and family on our fiftieth wedding anniversary. Instead, I was disappointed to find myself surrounded by other single ladies with a chip addiction and lack of hygiene. Besides the middle-aged manager, the closest contender for my new husband was a pimply-faced college student who bagged groceries. He moved as far away from me as possible, clearly letting me know that he found me repulsive. Meh. His loss.

When I realized the sirens were blaring at the Hubs' birthday dinner, I tried to be cool and figure out if there was a tornado bearing down on us or if this was one of those C.Y.A. alarms. I didn't want to frighten my children (who get the same training I did about deadly flying debris and farm animals), so I sauntered casually to the front of the restaurant where I could see out a window. The rain was coming down so hard and the wind was whipping every-thing, there could be a tornado outside the door and you wouldn't know it. I asked the teenage hostess, "Are the tornado sirens going off? Have you heard them?"

She giggled, "Yeah, they've been going off for a while."

I looked out the window again into the darkness and thought I saw a cow whiz by the glass. My mistake, it was just a piece of newspaper. Still. It was getting fierce out there. This wasn't a C.Y.A. siren. Shit was getting real.

"Okaaaay, so is there a tornado shelter here? Is there some place we should all go?" I put on my "mom face." You know the one. It's the one the says: Figure this shit out, kid. Oh, and you shouldn't be standing in front of glass doors, because I've seen enough disaster movies to know that you'll end up sliced to ribbons when the tornado comes through here. You're definitely an extra whereas, my family and I are the stars of this particular disaster movie. We'll survive this, but you won't, because you giggled at death.

The "mom face" worked. "Let me ask my manager," she said, scurrying away from the glass doors of death.

Good idea.

I followed her and found the manager huddled with the staff looking at weather apps on their phones. I have cheap mobile service (of course I do), so the internet wasn't working too well for me and I couldn't get the stupid news site to pop up. However, I could get Facebook. So, I asked the good people of Facebook to give me a weather update and tell me if I should seek shelter or keep eating my delicious chicken spiedini.

While I waited for the Book of Face to tell me what to do, the manager placated me by telling me that his boss was watching the weather and they'd get us in the kitchen if the storm sent tornadoes our way. I explained that I could hear the sirens and sirens meant imminent death. He said that they weren't the closest sirens. That was why they were so faint. They weren't for us. They were for other parts of town. He assured me that I could finish my chicken spiedini while houses ten blocks over flew off their foundations. He encouraged me to stay as long as I wanted to and to enjoy the hospitality of the restaurant and his staff. "No rush," he assured me. As if I could leave! I couldn't even see my car in the parking lot the rain and winds were so heavy. I just wanted him to announce it was an open bar. I think FEMA should totally pay for open bars during potential-almost-near-miss disasters.

I returned to my seat and filled in the adult members of my family. We'd continue to eat our celebratory dinner like the end of the world wasn't happening outside the (flimsy) walls of the restaurant.

What else could we do? We were better off where we were than inside a car.

We plastered fake smiles on our faces and assured my mother-in-law that this sort of thing happens "all the time" and she shouldn't worry even though all my friends on Facebook were telling me that people were reporting twisters touching down all around us.

"Who wants ice cream?" I asked. I got two scoops just in case this was the last time I ate ice cream. At least I'd go out with the taste of chocolate in my mouth.

We got ice cream and settled in to wait out the storm.

Pretty soon the world was blowing sideways outside the windows. That's when the manager announced that we'd all be heading to the kitchen now. I looked around to gather up my loved ones and my belongings and, of course, the Hubs was missing.

"Where's your son?" I asked my mother-in-law.

She shrugged. "I think the bathroom."

Of course he was in the bathroom at that very moment. Are you kidding me, Hubs?

It was like *Sophie's Choice*. Do I take my children and

go to the safety of the kitchen or go and find my husband in the toilet? I looked at my mother-in-law. Technically, the Hubs was her child and she should be the one to go and find him, but she's old and I should make sure that old people are safe. Besides she was the one leading the line to the kitchen. She's a New Yorker, not a Kansan. This was her first tornado and she wasn't going to take any chances.

Ugh. It was the Hubs' birthday dinner. I couldn't let him die on the crapper at his birthday dinner. I handed my children over to my mom and sent them to safety while I went to look for the Hubs. Lucky for me I didn't have to go far. He was right behind me. He must have just emerged from the bathroom and been looking around frantically for us before seeing the group going to the kitchen. "Oh thank goodness!" I said. "I was afraid I was going to have to go and find you in the Men's Room and we'd both have to hang on to urinals while the tornado tried to suck us away."

"Don't be ridiculous, Jen, I was finished with the bathroom ten minutes ago. I've been behind you the entire time. You didn't see me because you were too busy trying to decide if you should take your ice cream with you or leave it behind."

Oh. He saw that?

"Fine. I'm going to catch up to the kids." Translation: *How rude! I'll never try to hang onto a dirty urinal with you again! Save yourself next time!*

We filed into the kitchen where the floor was covered in water. Water was bubbling up from an overflowing grate in the floor.

HOLD ON A SECOND.

I don't mind being sucked out of a building or impaled by a tree branch. After spending the better part of my life in the Midwest, I've come to terms with that sort of death.

HOWEVER, I do not want to fall down a crevice in the Earth during an earthquake, be burned to ash in a forest fire, or drown during a tsunami. Drowning in a kitchen ranks right up there with tsunami. I am a Midwesterner. We only die in tornadoes or freak fireworks accidents.

"There's water coming out of the floor," I said to a worker.

"Yeah," he replied like I was the dumbest woman in the world. Sure, it was a dumb thing to say, but WATER WAS COMING OUT OF THE FLOOR.

I looked around for a fire exit. Surely there must be a door somewhere back there. I was not going to drown! I kept an eye on the water and watched to see if it would rise. The minute my shoes were covered, I was going to grab my kids and bolt through the back door. Luckily, the water never even got close to where I was standing.

I turned my attention to a more immediate danger: an enormous pot of pasta boiling on a stove top. I kept my kids as far away from that as possible. We weren't going to drown AND burn. *Carbs will kill me someday, but not today!*

We huddled in the kitchen while the waitstaff took selfies. (Seriously, they did. It was kind of funny.) I noticed one waiter holding a bundle that looked like a newborn baby. I watched him cradle his arms and hold his precious cargo tightly. *Who would give the waiter a baby to hold?* I wondered. *So weird.*

We waited.

The pot boiled.

The water gurgled from the drain, but didn't rise above just making the floor wet and slick (there was probably another drain nearby that was sucking it away). I had a better chance of dying from slipping on the floor and cracking my head open than drowning.

More selfies were taken.

Facebook statuses were updated. Including my own. I draw the line at near-death selfies, but I would update my Facebook status from the gallows.

Gomer asked, "Mom, is there anything I should be worried about?"

I hugged him and said, "Yeah. You should worry your ice cream will be melted when we get out of here."

Adolpha whined (of course), "How much longer?"

"Adolpha, go stand by your father."

After several more minutes passed with nothing happening, the manager decided we were out of danger and we were given the all-clear. We filed slowly out of the kitchen and as I passed the waiter holding the newborn baby, I said, "Do you have a baby in there?"

He smiled. "No," he said. "I have all the sharp objects."

Yeah, he was holding all of the butcher knives wrapped in towels and cloth napkins.

Before I could stop myself, I said, "Wow, your boss must really hate you," I said. "That's a shitty job to get."

He stopped smiling.

What? It *is* a shitty job!

Seriously, how much must the boss hate this guy to be like, "Billy, a tornado's coming and we need to make sure everyone in the restaurant is safe. I'll get everyone in the kitchen, you grab all the knives so when the tornado hits they won't fly around the kitchen and stick me. I mean, our very important patrons."

How about maybe you put them in a drawer next time?

We sat back down at our table where my mother-in-law re-thought her plan to move to the Midwest, my mother hoped our bill would be comped due to our "harrowing experience," Gomer slurped his soupy ice cream, and I checked Facebook to make sure the tornadoes weren't where we were headed. Once our bill was not comped, but instead paid by my dad, we took off so we go home and die in our own basement and not some flooded restaurant kitchen.

Happy Birthday, Hubs! Hope it was a good one! Next year my parents need to cook!

CHAPTER 11

I DREAMED OF GRASS (THAT DID NOT EXCEED FOUR INCHES IN HEIGHT PER THE CITY GUIDELINES)

THE HUBS WAS RAISED in New York City and for several years while we dated I lived there too. However, I was raised in the suburbs and after a couple of years the shine on the big city started to wear thin. The city had done me in. In one week I'd bought a loaf of bread at the grocery store that was home to a mouse, I'd been accosted on a subway train by a flasher, and a freak rain storm had washed me and all of the trash from the gutter on Fifth Avenue down a flight of stairs.

My job was stressful. I worked long hours and spent another couple of hours each day commuting. The Hubs and I wanted to get married and have kids, but I wasn't sure when I'd see them awake. It was very apparent that my job and kids did not mix, there wasn't one woman in my department with a child.

I lived in an apartment that cost more than the mortgage payment on my parent's four-bedroom house. My expensive apartment was one block from what I'm pretty sure was the most active fire station in all of New York City. Every twelve to fifteen minutes the sirens were blaring and the firemen were running off to save someone from certain death. While I appreciated their bravery and the service they provided, there were many nights that I wondered if maybe, just maybe, they could rush to be heroes just a smidge bit quieter? All I'm saying is were the sirens *that* necessary at three in the morning?

Every day was a battle and I was tired of battling. I knew that life in the suburbs wouldn't be like this. Sure the suburbs are its own special nightmare with nosy neighbors and competi-moms, but it wasn't *so* tough. In all my years of suburban dwelling, I'd never bought a loaf of bread with a resident mouse inside of it, the douchey dads at the neighborhood pool never flashed their junk at me, and I would have a car to shield me from the rain, the sun, the smog—all of the elements! The suburbs weren't hard. Or dirty. Or expensive. Or loud. (Although I'm sure even in the suburbs it's loud when you live near a fire station.)

It was weird, because I'd spent my teenage years dreaming of getting away from this particular cul-de-sac of hell. But the older I got, fresh air, low crime rates, wholesale clubs, and cookie cutter houses in homeowner's association-approved colors like Buff, Sand, and Camel started calling me like a siren song.

Then I started dreaming about grass (that did not exceed four inches in height per the city guidelines) and drive-thru everythings. In the suburbs, the drive-thrus aren't just for fast food and banks anymore. They're for the library, the pharmacy, the dry cleaners, ice cream, and Starbucks too. In the 'burbs, walking is for pussies. I had visions of my unborn children frolicking in the neighborhood pool and riding bikes in the cul-de-sac. That's when I knew I wanted to move back to the land of McMansions, SuperTargets, and award-winning public schools.

I knew going back wouldn't be easy.

I'd be surrounded by overachieving moms who spent their days humble bragging about absolute bullshit first world problems. ("I am *sooo* exhausted from packing for our cruise! It's so hard to know what to take when you're going to be gone for two weeks.")

I'd have to listen to people call their cleaning ladies "maids" and their babysitters "nannies" just so they could pretend they had a "staff." They'd try and pressure me to do my grocery shopping in large, well-lit stores that call themselves "markets" and sell their "philosophy" along with their soy chips. I'd be judged by my purchases and whether or not I brought my own bags.

I would be forced to endure Facebook status updates about my neighbors' *ah-may-zing* crossfit workouts they barely fit into their jam-packed day at dawn, their award-winning children (since when is a participation trophy an award?), their organic, free-range, sugar-free, dairy-free, gluten-free, Paleo, whole food lunch that closely resembled weeds, and pictures of manicures. God, the manicures! What is that all about? Who gives a shit what color you painted your nails?

Although I knew I'd be judged by the neighborhood I lived in, the stores I shopped, the car I drove, and the names I gave my children, I was confident I could hang.

I was willing to shell out the cash for a beige McMansion, because one of the only perks of living in suburbia is having four thousand affordable square feet you can fill with shit you don't need from big box stores. The only acceptable suburbanite cruising vessels are minivans and SUVs and since I've yearned for a minivan even before I had kids to put in it, I figured I had that covered. The only problem I was going to have was naming my future kids.

City dwellers like to give their kids stupid—I mean unique —names too. Like Astrid and Archie. But suburbanites are a whole different breed. They like to take normal names and then just butcher the hell out of them. Like Aighmey or Jaxon. Or they take random words and call them names, like Liberty or Branch. I knew I'd be judged harshly for my future children's names. I'd never be able to give my kids stupid—I mean unique—names like Nayvie and Rocco. I wasn't worried. I decided the name thing would actually come in handy. I would be able to judge my ability to bond with a mother by her child's name. If I met a Kinlee or a Tyberyus at the park, I'd know to steer clear of their mothers.

Although the odds were slim that I'd find a tribe of people I could get along with, I was willing to take the chance. I couldn't share another loaf of bread with a mouse or look at another crusty penis again. I couldn't work up a sweat fighting my way onto the subway each morning to get to a job that I hated. I couldn't marry the Hubs and have kids and then never see them. It was time to go.

I started putting the bug in the Hubs' ear. "It's sunny in Kansas City today. We could live on a golf course," I whispered into his ear one miserable Saturday morning. "You could tee off from our back porch."

"Why would I want to do that?" the Hubs asked.

"I don't know. I thought you'd like that idea. Doesn't it sound great?" I asked.

"Not really. Because if I can tee off our back porch, then that means everyone else can too. I don't want a bunch of asshole golfers traipsing through our backyard. Plus, if we're that close to the golf course, we're going to get a golf ball through one of our windows. No. I don't want to live on a golf course."

Good grief! I tried again. "Fine! We don't have to live on a golf course. There are plenty of other options. How about we live close to a park or a school?"

"I guess so. Just so long as it isn't too loud."

Too loud? Was he kidding me? Did he not hear the fire trucks every ten minutes?

"I'm sure there are plenty of quiet options," I said. "Like land. We could buy an acreage and not have any neighbors."

"An acreage?" the Hubs squealed. "You know how I feel about wide open spaces! I practically had a panic attack when we went to Maine last year. It was so dark and so uninhabited. I've never felt so alone and vulnerable in my life. I might not like my neighbors, but I want to be close enough to see in their windows."

As we walked home from our local, dingy (mouse-infested) grocery store one cold and rainy day, I tried to entice him again, "In the suburbs, there are huge, bright, clean grocery stores where you can drive up and they load your groceries into your car for you."

"Why do they do that?" the Hubs asked. "What's in it for them?"

"I don't know. They just do," I replied, impatiently. Why was he asking so many questions? Why wouldn't you want to shop at bright clean grocery store that loads your groceries for you? Why must he always be suspicious of everyone's ulterior motives?

"Can't you just wheel the cart of groceries to your car?" he asked.

"Yes, but when it's cold or rainy or snowy, wouldn't you like to park and have someone load your stuff for you?" I said.

"Do I have to tip the guy who loads my car?"

I was exasperated. This conversation was not going the way I'd hoped. "I don't know. Maybe."

"It actually sounds like a bit of a hassle," he said. "I bet there's always a line to get your groceries loaded, isn't there?"

I couldn't say, because I'd actually never done it. When you're single and you only buy one bag of groceries at a time, there isn't much need to use the drive-thru. Plus, there *was* always a line of people waiting to get their stuff and it did seem like a bit of a hassle. Damn him and his common sense reasoning! "But, isn't it nice to know that it's available if you ever wanted to do that?"

"Yeah, I guess so."

I tried a different tactic. I had been playing the wrong angle the whole time. The Hubs isn't swayed by creature comforts or cleanliness. Only money will move him.

"For what my rent costs, we could have a four bedroom house," I said triumphantly. *Boom.* Argue that one, Hubs!

His interest was piqued. "Oh yeah?"

"Oh. Yeah. We'd have plenty of room for us and a couple of kids and still pay less than what I pay now."

"Hmm. Would it have central air?"

"I wouldn't buy a house without it," I said, hoping he didn't ask me about the cost to run that central air, because as far as I was concerned it wasn't up for debate. The summers in Kansas are hot and humid, so running the air conditioner is not a luxury, it's a necessity. I'd eat ketchup sandwiches for the entire month of August to pay for the air conditioning bill.

"Central air. Nice," he murmured. I could see him coming around. He was starting to hear the siren song now. There's nothing like affordable square footage and amenities to gets the Hubs' heart pumping.

I decided to up the ante. "Our house would have an electric garage door opener. We'd just push a button an drive in. We'd never get wet again unloading the car." His eyes shone like a kid on Christmas. I continued, "In fact, we'd have openers on *all* three of our doors. "

"Wait. What? We'd have three garages?" the Hubs asked incredulously. "Why do we need three garages?"

"Well, as you know, there isn't much public transportation, so we'd each need a car. There's two bays and the third garage would be for bikes and stuff and, of course, our lawnmower."

At the mention of a lawnmower, the Hubs' eyes—that had moments before been dancing—went cold and lifeless. "I would have to mow our yard?" he asked.

"Well ..." I stammered, trying to think fast. "Yes. I mean, my dad usually did it. My mom did it if he was out of town and it was too long and we were going to get fined—"

"Fined? What are you talking about?" I was losing him!

Shit. I'd gone too far. Mayday! Mayday! He was never going to come to the Dark Side with me now.

I took a deep breath. "So ... Every neighborhood has a Homeowner's Association—the HOA. They dictate how long your grass can be, what color you can paint your house, if you can have a basketball goal in your driveway, that sort of thing."

"It's *my* yard. Maybe I like it long and weedy."

"Oh no, it doesn't work that way."

"Are you kidding me? Do these people have lives?"

"Yes, but they take their role on the HOA board very seriously. Also, if they drop the ball, there is always the city. The city measures your grass too. If it's too long, they go ahead and cut it and then fine you a hundred bucks or something."

"That's total bullshit," said the Hubs. "Why would anyone want to live in a place like that?"

"Well, for one, because it's pretty," I said. "There are neutral-colored houses instead of ones like that salmon-colored one over there." I pointed at the eyesore on the other side of the street. "Also, you might like your grass long and weedy, but no one else does. The basketball goal thing seems a little extreme to me, but I doubt it will be problem since our combined genes are never going to produce a baller."

"I'm thinking about it. I mean I like the idea of the garages and the space. And I'm even curious to know more about living on a golf course. If we lived far enough back, we probably wouldn't get a ball through the window. But these HOAs. They sound awful. If we move to the suburbs I never want to move to a neighborhood with these HOA assholes."

"Uh huh. We'll see," I said, making a mental note to start searching that night for homes with HOAs. He was ready to go.

He might talk tough, but I knew it was just easier to agree with the Hubs at that point, because he was full of shit. Deep down he likes things to be orderly and attractive too. He doesn't like salmon-colored houses anymore than I do or campers parked in neighbor's driveways or Christmas lights dangling from a house in July and the HOA is what makes sure that doesn't happen.

Within a year we were living in an HOA-governed neighborhood. We ponied up the dough for a dune-colored four bedroom, three bath house with automatic garage doors a couple of blocks from the elementary school. We paid our dues and enjoyed our community pool and all of the social events.

Sure you have to put up with the occasional petty bull-shit when you want to paint your front door red and you didn't get the architectural committee's approval before you painted it and so you get thirty registered letters asking you to please fill out the paperwork so the HOA can retroactively approve your red fucking door that is totally within the guidelines and shouldn't be such an issue but suddenly it is because you didn't do things in order and these people have no life except to manage everyone else's life. But the pluses outweigh the cons. My house maintains its value because if my neighbor's grass is too weedy or their dog is barking all day or their Christmas lights are still blinking in February, I can call the HOA and get that shit sorted without having to talk to my neighbor face to face.

Luckily, we have never had a run-in with the HOA. That's because we make sure to always pay someone to keep our grass at the mandatory four inches. I'll risk a red door, I'll build an unapproved deck, or put up an illegal basketball goal, but I'm afraid to mess around with the length of my grass. Because nothing makes the HOA go gangster on you faster than non-regulation length grass.

CHAPTER 12

PERVS, NUT TAPS, AND BODY SPRAY. OH MY! BUT AT LEAST HE SHOWERED?

WHEN I WAS eight I went away to sleep away camp for the first time. I was terrified. My mom and dad helped me find my cabin. It was empty and I could see where other girls had claimed their area by rolling out sleeping bags and placing toiletry bags on shelves. All that was left was a top bunk. I'd never slept on a top bunk, but I was excited to try. My mom was reluctant. She had reason to be. I've always been a bit of a cluster. I fall down walking on level surfaces, so of course I would fall out of a top bunk. She was certain I'd fall out of bed when I thrashed in the night, but she could also picture me falling out of my bed in broad daylight while trying to see the time on my wrist watch. In her mind I'd spend more time on the floor of my cabin than in my bed. I could see her going through the worst-case scenarios in her head and I waited for her to sweep Muffy's adorable gingham sleeping bag off the bottom bunk and take it for herself. But she didn't do that. She sighed heavily and said, "We should have gotten here earlier."

"The traffic was awful," my dad complained. "There was nothing I could do."

"It will be fine. Jenni, just sleep on your back and try to never roll over," my mom advised.

They got me settled onto my top bunk with my (not adorable gingham) sleeping bag and my personalized "Jenni" pillow. My parents said good bye to me. I told them I was going to go down to the pool with the other kids and get to know some of my bunk mates. I was totally lying. I was never going to walk into a crowd of strangers and introduce myself. Instead I climbed up on my bed, opened one of the thirty books I'd brought with me and ate Twizzlers. I scarfed candy, read, and cried a little. (Still some of my favorite things to do, BTW. Who doesn't love a comfy bed, a great book, some Twizzlers, and a good cleansing cry?) I'm not sure how long I stayed there. In my eight-year-old mind it seemed like half the day, but based on the quantity of licorice I ate, I'm going to say it was half an hour before my counselor, Ingrid, came looking for me. She coaxed me out of my bed like I was a reluctant stray cat. I already had licorice, so she couldn't convince me to come down from my bunk for candy. I'm not sure how she got me out of bed, but she did. I climbed down, snuffling the whole way, and wiped my nose on my arm.

She put her arm around me and said, "It's okay, Jenni, we're going to have so much fun!"

At the time I didn't believe a word she said. I was positive the week would suck and I would die from some rare disease caused by too many mosquito bites or not enough hugs from my mom. That's if I didn't die first from falling on my head from my top bunk. I wasn't the outdoorsy type and even at eight I wasn't one of those rah-rah types who would drink the proverbial Kool-Aid and join in and be a happy little camper singing Kumbaya and making God's Eyes by the bushel.

But somehow the week didn't suck at all and I give all the credit to Ingrid. She was a college student, but to me she seemed as authoritative as my mother, but so much more fun. Like on "Backwards Day" not only did she wear her clothes backwards, she wore them inside out *and* backwards and then walked backwards all day and ate her food backwards (dessert first). My mother would never wear her clothes backwards or eat dessert first. It just wasn't done. Ingrid didn't care. At night she would tell us ghost stories that were just scary enough to send chills down our spine, but not too scary that we couldn't sleep. She could French braid like a magician and every morning she whipped ten little girls' hair into matching braids. She was The Coolest Counselor and I felt lucky to be in her presence. Although Ingrid was amazeballs, she didn't let us get away with stuff. We won the "Cleanest Cabin" award every day and she would squash any sort of girly cattiness as soon as she saw it starting to take off. She'd tug on our braids and tell us that this was our first year of camp and we were going to be friends for the rest of our lives, so we needed to treat each other kindly.

I don't have a lot of happy childhood memories, but thanks to Ingrid, some of my fondest memories are of my time spent at camp. Once I had children, I knew that I would send my kids away to camp too. I never thought it would be a problem. So when Gomer was eight, I was fully prepared to send him. I told him I was packing him off to camp. He mulled it over and said, "No, thank you."

Wait. What? I could have said "No" when I was a child? I never even thought of saying "No" to my parents. They just packed me up and dropped me off. There was no discussion! What just happened? Then I saw that I'd made the classic mistake of making Gomer think he had a choice in the matter. I quickly decided I would do as my parents did and ship Gomer off. End of discussion.

But then I panicked.

Although he's my first born, he was still my baby. He looked so little standing there begging me not to send him away. "Please, Mommy, I don't want to be away from you," he said, softly. Instead of remembering all the fun I had with Ingrid and my new friends, I thought of the little girl crying in her bunk and gorging herself on Twizzlers. I caved in and let Gomer stay home; safely nestled in my bosom.

The next summer I didn't even ask Gomer if he wanted to go to camp. Truthfully, I didn't want him to go away. I am a chronic worrier and the thought of him accidentally drowning during swim time or dying from a bee sting (even though he was an excellent swimmer and had no history of being allergic to bees) was too much for me. I wouldn't be able to sleep with him away from me. I nestled him into my bosom again and didn't even tell him about camp sign ups.

Another summer came around and by then Gomer was ten. A few friends asked me if he was going to camp. I said, "Oh no! Gomer doesn't want to go. He'd rather be home with me and the Hubs."

My friends looked surprised. "Really?" asked Mathilda. "Oscar loves camp. It's his favorite part of summer."

"Yes," agreed Annalise. "Friedman plans all year long for camp. He can't get enough of it."

I shrugged my shoulders. "I don't know what to say. It's just not for Gomer." *Or me,* I thought.

It was about a week before camp and Gomer asked me, "Hey Mom, remember that camp you wanted to send me to a couple years ago?"

"Yes?"

"Well, I was talking to Oscar and he said it's really fun."

"Oh yeah?" I asked, casually.

"Yeah. Friedman likes it too."

"Well, good for them. I'm glad they enjoy it," I said.

"Do you think I could go this year?"

"Hmm, I don't know. It starts in a week. I bet there isn't any room. Maybe next year."

Gomer looked sad. "Do you think you could call and check? Maybe there was a cancellation and there is room for me now?" he suggested.

Why is my kid so damn smart? I wondered.

"Sure. I'm a little busy right now, but I can try calling them later today." *After the office is closed.*

"I brought you the phone and I found the number online."

Damn you, Google, and your wealth of knowledge you put at my child's fingertips!

"Oh, super. Thanks, honey."

"Maybe you could take a break and just call them real fast?"

There was no avoiding it. My child was looking at me with such hope in his eyes. I almost said, "Or we could just cuddle, Pumpkin." I thought better of it and picked up the phone and dialed.

The phone rang twice and a cheery voice answered. I introduced myself and said, "I'm calling about the camp you're hosting next week. My son, Gomer, was interested in going. He's never been. I'm sure it's full. So, never mind, maybe we'll try next year."

"Are you kidding? A first timer? We'd love to have him! We've got always got room for one more!" the woman on the phone said.

I was surprised. "Oh! Wow. That's good news. I'm sure there's a huge late fee I need to pay though," I said, frowning at Gomer. Gomer knew the Hubs would be too cheap to pay the late fee. I could practically hear the sad trombones wailing, *Wah-wah*.

"Nope! Not at all. I simply need you to fill out the paperwork and pay us before the end of business today and he'll be all set."

"Oh. Well, I'm pretty busy, but I'll try and get it all done in time," I said.

"Even if you can't get it to me before tomorrow, Jen, it will be fine. I've got him on the list and if I don't get your information today, I'll give you a call tomorrow and remind you. I'll make sure we get him in!"

No matter what I said, this perky camp director was determined to get my kid in her clutches. I finally gave up and said, "Okay, sounds good. Thanks for your help."

"You bet! I can't wait to meet Gomer!"

I hung up the phone. "Go get my credit card, please, Gomer," I said, sadly.

He ran out of the room whooping and hollering.

The week leading up to camp was a scramble to get him all of the "camp essentials" like bug spray, new under-wear (because he didn't have enough clean ones to make it through the week and I wasn't in the mood to do laundry before he left), a flashlight, and enough snacks to feed his entire cabin for the week because I remembered camp food always sucked. I had to speak at a conference the weekend he was leaving, so I wouldn't be the one drop-ping him off at camp. I made sure I packed Gomer's bag before I left. The only things the Hubs had to remember to throw in the car was Gomer and his pillow. I wasn't sure I could trust him with that simple task, so I put a

Post-It Note on the door to the garage: TAKE GOMER'S PILLOW!!

I got home from my conference and immediately assaulted The Hubs with a barrage of questions: Did Gomer cry? Has he called? Has the camp called? Did Gomer seem sad? Did the Hubs notice any bees when he dropped him off? Did the Hubs kiss him? Did he remember the pillow?

The Hubs answered me: No, of course not. No, of course not. No, of course not. No, of course not. No, of course not. A hug is as good as a kiss. Yes, I'm not a total idiot.

For the next few days I sat around wondering if Gomer was okay. Was he having fun? Did he make some friends? Was he crying in his (top) bunk each night? Had he wandered off into the woods and gotten lost and no one even noticed yet that he was missing?

The week passed and it was time to pick Gomer up from camp. I told the Hubs I wanted to go alone to get him. "Why?" the Hubs asked me.

"Because I know him and I know you. He'll have a lot to tell us about camp and you'll tell him he's talking too much. I want to hear how it was and I want the truth. He'll censor himself around you."

The Hubs looked offended for about half a second and then shrugged and said, "Well, honestly, the kid won't shut up. How many stories about canoeing or fish he never caught can we listen to? You coddle him, Jen!"

"I don't coddle him," I argued. "I listen to him. I let him tell me about his experiences. What do you know? You didn't even kiss him goodbye!"

"Because he's ten and when I asked if he wanted a kiss he said no!"

"You don't ask if he wants a kiss. You just give them!"

"Fine. Go by yourself," the Hubs said.

A few hours later I arrived at the campgrounds and found a large group of parents gathered outside the main building. "What's going?" I asked one of the mothers.

"They're not quite done signing everyone's camp logs," she said. "So we're waiting out here."

"Oh," I replied. I thought about going inside the building. It had been over a week since Gomer had last seen me. I was sure he was missing me desperately and watching the clock. I didn't want him to be upset and think I was "late" when really I was outside the whole time waiting for him to finish up. After a few more minutes, I decided to go ahead and go inside and see my baby—errr, I mean I my son. I cracked open the door to the building and peeked around the corner. I was greeted by a horde of wilding children. They were screaming and flying up and down the long hallway trying to get everyone's signature on their camp log. "Sign mine! Sign mine!" they screamed. One little girl even stopped and handed me a Sharpie. "Sign it," she ordered.

"I didn't go to camp," I stammered.

She shrugged. "It's okay. Sign it anyway."

I scribbled my name on her book and looked around for Gomer. I checked the corners first since that's where I'd be sulking at his age (and my current age). I didn't see him. I checked the bathroom (another favorite hiding spot of mine). He wasn't there either.

A counselor came up to me. "Hi, can I help you find someone?" she asked.

"Yes. I'm looking for Gomer?" I phrased it as a question, because I wasn't sure she'd know who Gomer was. If he was anything like his mother, he blended in so well with the wallpaper that no one ever noticed him.

"Oh! You're Gomer's mom!"

"Yes. Do you know him?"

"Of course! He's an amazing kid." *Why yes he is.* "He's so outgoing!"

"Gomer?"

She laughed. "Yes! Let's see if I can spot him." She looked around the busy room. "There he is!" She pointed to a child who couldn't possibly be mine. He was enormous. He was at least three inches taller than Gomer and he was much broader than Gomer. Also, he had a terrible haircut. He was practically bald.

"Umm ...," I said, as the boy turned around and I could see his face.

"Mom!"

"Oh my! That *is* my kid," I said. "Thanks!"

"Mom!" Gomer waved me over.

"Gomer!" I leaned in for a hug and a kiss and he immediately threw up a block.

"Mom!" he complained.

"Sorry, honey. I just missed you a lot," I said. "Did you have fun."

"Tons."

"Great. Was the food terrible?" I asked.

"No! It was awesome. We cooked hot dogs in the fire and baked pizza on tortilla shells. Can we make that for dinner tonight?"

Ewww. No. "Maybe." I smoothed his non-existent hair. "What happened to your hair?"

"Oh yeah, you were gone. I forgot. Dad took me to get a haircut the night before camp."

"But why so short?" Gomer's hair had never been so short. I could see his scalp.

"You said I had to wash my hair every day and Dad said

if I cut it short I can soap it up with the rest of my body."

"I see," I said. I made a mental note to congratulate the Father of the Year. "Are you about ready to go? I thought we could stop for lunch on the way home and you could tell me all about camp!"

Gomer said, "Yeah, just a few more minutes. I want to get some more signatures on my camp log." Gomer took off and left me standing there alone.

Mathilda walked over. "At least he had fun," she said, sympathetically.

"It's like I don't even know him," I said. "He didn't let me kiss him ... he's bigger ... and that haircut ..."

"The haircut is the worst," Mathilda agreed. "Last year Oscar had a tick on his head that we didn't notice until a week after camp. At least if Gomer has a tick you'll see it right away."

"How did it go?" Annalise came up.

"A little too well I think," Mathilda said.

"Gomer didn't miss his mommy?"

"You remember that, don't you, Annalise?" Mathilda said, sadly.

"Oh yeah," Annalise nodded.

Just then Gomer came up and put his arms around me. "Okay. I'm ready to go, Mom," he said.

I grinned evilly at Mathilda and Annalise. Maybe their boys didn't miss their mommy, but mine certainly did! Gomer might look strange with his stupid haircut and maybe he seemed a little bigger and he might not have wanted to kiss me in front of his new friends, but deep down he was still my little boy (and the hair would grow out).

Gomer and I walked to the car with our arms around one another's shoulders. "Did you miss me?" I whispered.

"Sure," he said. It wasn't quite a "Yes," but it would suffice.

I was congratulating myself on raising such a sweet little boy and convincing myself that I had several more years left where Gomer would hug me and miss me, when Gomer asked, "Hey Mom, what's humping?"

I choked on my spittle. "Humping?" I repeated. "Where did you learn that word?"

"From Oscar. He likes to hump his bed. It's kind of weird."

"I see."

"Why is he doing that? Our counselor kept calling him a perv when he'd do that. What's a perv?"

Jesus. What the hell kind of camp did I send my kid to?

"Oh and do you know what a nut tap is?" he asked.

"No. I have no idea what that is." My mind raced. "Gomer. Did someone touch your nuts? You remember learning about good touches and bad touches? Did someone bad touch you, Gomer?" Oh. My. God. Was my child molested at camp? Did someone touch his privates?

"No." Gomer said. "It's not bad touches, Mom. Yuck! What's wrong with you? It's just guys having fun."

"So, nut tapping is fun?"

"Yeah, our counselor, Matt—he was the coolest coun-selor—would tap our nuts when we were acting like jerks. Not hard-hard, but kind of hard. He taught us you've always gotta protect your nuts, Mom."

"Uh huh." Humping, pervs, nut taps? My snowflake was melting. Who the hell was this kid? It was like I didn't even know him. What had I done? I thought the week would be fun and instead he'd lost his innocence. I tried to remember back to my days as a camper. Did I come home talking about such things or was this a boy thing?

"Hey Mom. Have you ever heard of Axe body spray? My counselor, Matt, wears it. I totally need some body spray. We used so much of Matt's this week that he said if we don't bring our own next year he will nut tap us."

Yup. It's a boy thing. Someone hold me I am not ready for this stage.

CHAPTER 13

DIETS SUCK BALLS

AS YOU MAY or may not know, I'm a fluffy girl. I've been a round little nugget for most of my life. I'm always looking for a new diet to fail at and this year I was not disappointed. Before this, I'd been doing that diet where you're supposed to throw out your scale and eat what your body tells you to eat. Remember that stupid fucking diet? Yeah, well I was doing that one. And guess what my body was telling me to eat? Donuts mostly. But I really hoped that the occasional craving for a carrot would balance it all out. Guess what? It did not. I finally climbed back on the scale only to be greeted with the biggest number in my life. I weighed more than I did when I was pregnant! WTF? I was miserable. I was living in sweatpants because nothing else fit and I hated myself. Problem is, guess what I do when I'm miserable and I hate myself? If you said eat donuts, you'd be right. So, of course, I went into a shame spiral of eating more because I hated how fat I'd become and shockingly it didn't help the number on the scale go down.

The Hubs knew I was feeling like shit so he showed me a website he thought I should try. It was one of those miracle diets where they promise you that you'll lose twenty to forty pounds in a month a half. "It's only a month and a half," the Hubs said. "You'd feel better and you'd be happier if you did this. I'll help you."

So, the next day I found myself in the doctor's office listening to the spiel about this wonder diet. The information was very vague with lots of exclamation points and you-can-do-its coming out of the mouths of the believers. I was desperate. I'd reached a new low ... err, a new high ... and I had to do something drastic. So I forked over the cost of a mortgage payment and signed on the dotted line.

That's when the true secret of the diet was revealed to me: a super duper calorie-restricted diet that did not include salt, sugar, dairy, wheat, oil, alcohol, or processed anything for the next forty days. Basically I was going to eat hunks of grass-fed meat with dry lettuce and an organic apple.

I went home and cried. "There's no way I can do this!" I wailed to the Hubs.

He was already online searching for recipes that he could make me. "You can. I told you, I'll help you."

He wasn't lying ... sort of. You see, the Hubs thinks it's helping me when he cooks me three ounces of wild buffalo seasoned with only garlic and onions. And he's right, that is helpful. He also thinks it's helpful when he encourages me to leave the house. That is not helpful. Where would I go? Clothes shopping? Please. This is not my first diet. I've got the next three sizes covered. The grocery store? I wasn't going to go near that fucking minefield where actual forbidden fruit (like bananas) would serenade me like sirens and drive me into their yellow arms. (At least it wasn't donuts calling my name anymore.)

The first three weeks of my diet, I stayed home and never left the house. I was more depressed than before. I have always equated food with socializing. I meet my girl-friends for lunch or drinks. We don't meet to go for walks through the park and trade salt-free recipes for free-range chicken. I didn't want to go anywhere, because I was tempted by food. The Hubs thought this was stupid. He thought I should take a shower and get dressed (in smaller pants) and go out and live my life.

"It could be fun walking down the aisles of Whole Foods to see if there's a new salt-free, sugar-free spice you can have," he said.

"Fuck you," I replied. "Even Whole Foods has dessert. I want dessert."

"Easy, Jen, it must be getting close to lunch time. I feel you're a bit hangry."

"Fuck you."

I resisted going anywhere for days, but finally one day I couldn't avoid it. This fantastical diet had promised to reset my metabolism, refresh my hormones, realign my chakras, and make me funnier. Okay, I exaggerate a little bit, you get my drift. EVERYTHING was going to change for me.

Well, let me tell you, EVERYTHING did change for me. After eight blissful years, I woke up to a long-forgotten sensation: menstrual cramps. I've had IUDs since Adolpha was born and one of the lovely side effects is that I never get a period anymore.

"What the hell?" I muttered, climbing out of bed and heading to the bathroom. Sure enough, my motherfucking period was back. "Oh helllllll no!" I yelled.

"What? What is it?" the Hubs asked me, all concerned.

"I got my period!"

"Well, the doctor did say everything would change."

"Yeah, but my period? Shit," I said. *Shit ...* that word got me thinking. *How long has it been since I've done number two?* I wondered. I pushed that thought from my mind, because I didn't have time to worry about that bodily function, I had another one to deal with first. "I need to go to the store. I have no supplies anymore."

"Great!" the Hubs said. "We can swing by Costco too. You're out of cod."

Cod. Literally the grossest thing on my new and improved menu. I read somewhere that Dwyane "The Rock" Johnson eats cod for breakfast, lunch, and dinner. Cod is bad enough for dinner, I can't imagine gagging it down first thing in the morning. Good thing I don't want to be as buff as The Rock!

Before I knew it, I agreed to go to Costco. "Fine. But you're not getting a hot dog," I told him. "The hell I'm going to sit there and watch you eat a hot dog while I eat handfuls of spinach."

We walked into Costco and I realized that the Hubs brought us during "Sample Time." Now, I can't say he did this on purpose, but the Hubs does have a sixth sense for free food, so *some* part of his brain was aware of what he was doing.

"Hey," the Hubs said, with faux enthusiasm. "Why don't you look at the jeans section. I bet you can fit into some new jeans now! I'll go and find the cod."

I narrowed my eyes. The Hubs knows that I've got three different sizes of jeans in my closet. I didn't need anymore new jeans. But I'm not one to argue when he encourages me to buy stuff, so I headed over to check out what Gloria Vanderbilt had to offer Costco shoppers.

I wandered through the jeans, the sweaters, and the yoga pants. I threw boots and tennis shoes into my cart. After perusing the entire clothing and book section, I finally headed into the food section to see what was keeping the Hubs and my frozen cod.

"Cheese?" an elderly lady offered.

"Excuse me?" I asked.

"Would you like a sample of cheese? It's a mild cheddar on sale today."

I looked at the tray of little white squares with toothpicks sticking out of them and resisted the urge to hoover the entire lot. I have a theory that anything can be made tastier by dipping it in cheese or chocolate. My kids have a game where they're trying to stump me, but you can't. I'd slather cheese on anything —even cod. Since I'd been on the diet, I hadn't missed much, but cheese was something that called my name every single day.

"No, thank you," I said. I tried to be polite. It wasn't the old lady's fault that wanted to punch her in the throat for even offering me cheese.

As I walked away I was pretty sure I heard the little cheese squares calling out to me, "What an asshole! She should have totally eaten us. We're delicious." Fuck you, cheese!

"Spiral ham?" Another old lady offered.

An old man shoved a plate in my face. "Meatball?"

"Raisin bread?"

"Fettuccine Alfredo?"

ARGHHHH!!!

I had to find the Hubs and get out of Costco. I searched the aisle frantically looking for him. I didn't want to abandon my boots and tennis shoes, but I was about ready to text him to say I was going to the car. And then I spied him. He was lurking in snack aisles. He popped his head around a stack of granola bars and pulled it back quickly when he was saw me coming.

I rounded the corner and he had his back to me. "What are you doing?" I asked. "We've got to get out of here. I'm going to lose it."

"Umm ... okay," he mumbled, still not turning around.

"What is going on?" I demanded.

He turned slowly, guiltily and I could see chocolate in the corners of his mouth. He opened his hand to reveal a slightly melty chocolate, caramel, macadamia nut cluster. "You son of a bitch," I said.

"I didn't want you to see," he said. "Honestly, it's not even that good. The cheddar biscuits were so much better."

I wanted him to choke on the nut cluster. I wouldn't have let him die, but I would have let him come close before I Heimlich-ed him. "You check out. I'll meet you in the car," I seethed.

He looked at my cart. "Really, Jen, you need more shoes?"

I glared at him. "Yes, I really need more shoes. I earned them today."

While I waited for him, I added up how many days it had been since I'd had any movement from down under. It had been several. So many that I was a tad concerned. I called the doctor and he told me that it was a fairly normal thing for people on such a restricted diet, but that if I was feeling uncomfortable I could try a tea called Smooth Move.

"I'm sorry, did you say Smooth Move?"

"Yes, I did," he said, all business-like.

"Okay, just checking," I chuckled.

The Hubs and I finished our shopping in stony silence interrupted only by his juicy burps of cheese and chocolate. Asshole. I got my tampons and my tea.

That night I made a cup of Smooth Move tea and I

waited. And waited. And waited. Nothing happened. Until the next day.

The next day I was shopping in Walmart with Adolpha. She has been assigned yet another giant project that a third-grader is incapable of doing alone and so we were shopping for the necessary supplies. As we loaded our cart with Popsicle sticks, felt, glue sticks, and new Sharpies (because I needed a treat and new Sharpies are almost like gummy bears) I felt an odd sensation. A twinge. A slight movement. A little pressure. And then ...

"OH MY GOD!" I screamed.

"What, Mommy?" Adolpha asked me, terrified.

I looked around, panicked. If I didn't hurry, I was going to have my smooth move in the middle of the craft aisle. "Where is the closest bathroom?" We were in the middle of the store.

"The back is better," Adolpha said. "They're cleaner and there won't be a line."

"Let's go!" I ran like the wind. Seriously. I wish someone had video, because I haven't run that fast since I was ten probably.

Two nice young men were trying to get you to change your cable provider. They were steps away from the bathroom and so I'd have to pass them. "Excuse me, ma'am, can you please tell me who—"

"Don't talk to me!" I hollered, racing by. I needed every ounce of concentration I had to keep from crapping my pants.

I will say that I made it in time. I will also say that I'd like to apologize to Walmart for the damage that I did to their restroom. Luckily you guys sell air fresheners. I would recommend putting one in that restroom. I would also recommend putting a restroom in the middle of your fucking store.

This is the hardest diet I've ever been on, but I refuse to give up. I always give up. I always let myself fail. I won't do that this time. This time I'll finish. I might knock out an old lady for a bite of cheese. I might shit my pants in the middle of a store. I might kill my husband the next time he licks peanut butter off of a knife and tells me how delicious it is. But I WILL finish this diet and I'll look damn good when I'm on trial.

CHAPTER 14

IT'S NOT YOU, IT'S US

I WAS SCROLLING through my Facebook feed as I do every morning. I didn't see much that caught my eye other than a few Grumpy Cat memes (man, I love that cat!), a video of some weird woman dancing in Spandex pants, and someone looking for book recommendations. I gave the cat pics a thumbs up, I watched the video and left the comment, WTF did I just watch??, and I dropped no fewer than ten recommendations on the person looking for something new to read.

I scrolled a bit further and that's when I saw a picture of my friends, Gretchen and Sybil. They were in Sybil's kitchen, surrounded by several people I didn't recognize. Everyone was laughing and having a great time. The caption read: "So glad I could have my favorite people over for game night tonight!"

Now, I realized that I was a forty-three-year-old woman, but that picture took me right back to seventh grade. Right back to those Monday mornings where I'd hear a group of friends talking about the great time they had together sleeping over at someone's house. A party that I wasn't invited to.

It was like a punch in my gut to see this picture. I used to be invited to game night. Why wasn't I invited this time? I tried to remember when I stopped being invited. It had been quite awhile but I just assumed that Game Night had been disbanded. It appeared that I was wrong. I scrolled through Sybil's pictures and saw evidence of several get-togethers where I was left off the guest list.

I know I shouldn't have cared that Gretchen and Sybil got together without me. But I did care. I realized that Gretchen and Sybil hadn't called me in months. I tried to remember the last time I'd spoken to Gretchen or Sybil. It had been a few months. I was in the grocery store and I ran into Sybil. At the time it seemed normal enough. We both complained about how busy life was. How we were professional chauffeurs. We talked about getting together in the future, but neither of us pulled out our phones and made a date. After that I tried reaching out a few times and getting together. Every time I tried to get something planned with her or Gretchen, they were busy. The last time I had spoken to either of them was to invite them to my book launch.

Although I'd published books before, this was my first one with a Big Five publisher. It wasn't just a big deal to me, it was a big fucking deal. I was finally achieving a life long goal of mine. I asked Gretchen and Sybil to come. They said they wouldn't miss it for the world. They were happy for me. They were proud of me. I was nervous and terrified to speak to a large group of people I didn't know and it would be comforting to see a few familiar faces in the crowd.

On the day of the event, I texted them both to remind them. Gretchen replied first, "Oh darn! I had this on the calendar for weeks, but Bill made plans to go for happy hour with his buddies and we have no one to watch the kids."

Really, Bill? You had to go tonight with your buddies? You couldn't have gone last night or maybe go tomorrow night? It had to be tonight?

I wasn't sure how to reply. I didn't want to make a huge deal out of it, but on the other hand I didn't want Gretchen to think that I *wasn't* bothered. So I just wrote back. "That sucks. I would have loved to see you. I wish Bill would have checked the calendar."

She came back with, "What can you do?"

I don't know? Maybe tell your husband that you've had an event on the calendar for three months and you'd appreciate it if he'd go out with his drinking buddies next week? I mean, I guess you'd do that if you cared at all about your friend.

A few hours later Sybil replied to my text. "Sorry, it's my turn to drive carpool for soccer tonight. Have fun!"

Seriously??? This is probably one of the biggest nights of my life and she couldn't trade her carpool night to be there?

I didn't even reply to her. I just couldn't. I'd had it with the both of them.

It hurt me terribly. I went to all of their fucking things. I've been to ballet recitals, awards banquets, and home shopping parties. I've spent fortunes on their shit to support them and their business endeavors, but they couldn't take two hours out of their precious night to come and support me?

Fine. Message received. Loud and clear.

I stewed for a bit, but then I realized I was letting them ruin my day. I refused to let them get me down. I went to my launch and I had a wonderful night. I remember the friends who *were* there. Their presence meant more than they know. I won't forget them. I remember them all and I am so grateful to them and I will always try to support them in all that they do, even if it means switching my carpool night.

It's been a year now since I've spoken to or hung out with Gretchen and Sybil. We're still friends on Facebook and every now and again I will see a picture or a status update and I get a twinge of jealousy and sadness and wonder what went wrong. But a few weeks ago I read a list that a blogger wrote about why you're not friends with certain people anymore. There were suggestions like "Your Friend Entered a Committed Relationship" and "Your Friendship is Toxic." All three of us were in committed relationships when we met, so that didn't change and I didn't think our friendship was ever toxic. It wasn't like we got together to binge drink and shoplift every weekend. And then I read the suggestion: "You've Grown in Different Directions Over Time."

That was us. That's what happened to us.

When Gretchen and Sybil and I met, we all had little kids. We were stay-at-home moms looking for something— anything—to do with our rugrats and get us out of the house. Our kids were all the same ages and enjoyed playing with one another. We lived close to one another so it was easy to get together for a jaunt to the park or the local pool. We'd get together two or three times a week. Sometimes with the kids, sometimes as couples, and sometimes just us. But we started drifting apart after our kids entered school. They didn't attend school together or play sports together, so we had fewer reasons to see one another. We fought to hang on. We'd invite one another's kids to birthday parties and we'd get together on weekends, but it became increasingly harder to do so. For whatever reason, I either drifted away from the group or I was quietly pushed out.

My direction had veered onto a completely different path than theirs. By then I was writing full time and I was living a completely unconventional life. They didn't want to hear about my writer's block and had no idea how to respond when I'd complain about my trouble with some asshole who kept emailing me pictures of his junk. They couldn't understand why I'd write the things I did and air my dirty laundry for the world to laugh at. They couldn't believe that I'd spend hours every day alone in a room chained to a laptop—and loving it.

I didn't just go in a different direction, I went completely off the reservation. I didn't mean to, but I changed and they stayed the same. We no longer had anything in common and it was more of an inconvenience to stay friends.

I understand now that my time with Gretchen and Sybil is over. I'm not mad or sad that they're getting together without me. I'm not jealous or upset. They weren't mean to me or cruel to me. It's not like I think they're bitching about me over margaritas and a plate of nachos. In fact I don't think they think about me at all anymore, and if I'm being completely honest, that hurts more than losing them. I sometimes wonder if they even miss me. I don't think they do. I was a friend merely out of convenience and that fact can hurt if I let myself dwell on it.

I need to let them go and not be bothered by them anymore. I need to like their photos that don't include me. I need to focus on the friends who do get me and who understand me and who want to support me.

Not all friends are meant to stay in our lives forever. If you have one or two of those kinds of friends, then you're luckier than you know. It's hard to know who will be the "forever" friends and who will be the "right now" friends, but I have to treat every friend like they're a forever friend. I'm to blame too for growing apart from Sybil and Gretchen. It wasn't just them. I chose to put my career ahead of my friendships. I chose to distance myself from anyone who didn't "get" me and what I do. I could have done better and I didn't. There are other friends who I invest in, but for some reason I didn't invest in Sybil and Gretchen. Maybe I could feel it too, maybe I could tell that we weren't meant to be friends for a long time and that's why I didn't fight to keep the friendship going. I'm not sure, but I think it will be a reminder to me going forward. I need to do a better job cultivating friendships that are important to me. I say friends are important, but I need to show them that they're important.

I miss my friends who have disappeared over the years, but more importantly, I'm thankful for the friends who have gone in their different directions too, but still managed to maintain our friendship. Those are the real relationships in my life and those are the ones that I will always work hard to maintain and if I ever see one of those friends having a party I'm not invited to, I just might burn down the internet.

CHAPTER 15

WHY I'M NO LONGER A PROFESSIONAL HAND MODEL

THE HUBS and I are idiots. I'm not even exaggerating a little bit. Sometimes it's amazing that we get anything done, because we're so stupid. We both have the mindset of a twelve-year-old. We spend most of our time watching terrible reality television and giggling at fart jokes.

Remember that girl in grade school who would kick the boys in their shins? Remember what their parents told them about that girl? "She likes you. She's showing you that she likes you." Yeah, I'm that grade school girl who punches the boy she has a crush on.

Normally the Hubs doesn't care unless I get too violent. Like the time I bit him. I was irritated with him and he wouldn't shut up so I bit him. It wasn't a hard bite and it was through his shirt, but still. I bit him. Like a forty-three-year-old toddler throwing a temper tantrum. He was so shocked he wouldn't come around me for the rest of the day. I guess it worked!

Sometimes the Hubs and I get messing around—no, I don't mean sex—I mean "rastling." We start swatting each other and pushing each other. I don't know why. Don't ask me. We just do. He'll grab me and challenge me to break free and then I'll elbow him in the gut. As you can see, I'm always the violent one of the two of us. When your mom used to warn you not to mess around with your friends because "someone will get hurt" she was talking about me. I am always the one who kicks it up a notch but ends up hurting myself instead of the Hubs and that's when I get myself into even bigger trouble.

A few years ago it was late one night and the Hubs kept putting his icy cold feet on me. I hate feet in any condition, but icy cold and sweaty are both triggers for me to Hulk out. I started kicking his feet off me and I tried to push him out of our bed. He pushed back. We got tangled up and I gave him one more hard shove and off the bed he went. But because we were entwined, I went off the bed too. Because he's got cat-like skills, he landed easily on his feet laughing like a jack ass. Because I've got baby-hippo-like skills, I landed on my face, screaming with my hand mashed under me. When I finally managed to get to my feet we could see that my pinky was in bad shape. It was completely bent back and swelling up.

"Oh shit!" I exclaimed. "Look what you did to me!"

The Hubs continued laughing. "I didn't do that to you. You did it to yourself. You shouldn't have tried to push me on the floor."

"I wouldn't have pushed you on the floor if you hadn't put your cold feet on me," I wailed.

"I'll get you some ice," the Hubs offered. "Or I can put my foot on it."

He brought me ice, put on some socks, and jumped back into bed with me. "Are you okay now?"

"Yes," I whimpered.

"You're such a toughie. You're strong like bull." He grunted, cuddling up to me.

"Shut up."

"You'll be fine. Just keep the ice on your finger."

The next day the swelling had gone down, but my pinky still pointed in the wrong direction.

"I think I should go to the doctor," I said.

"Really, Jen? Are you that much of a baby? Your finger is fine. It's the most useless finger you have. You won't even miss it."

"You don't want me to go, because you're afraid of what it will cost," I said. At that very moment we were still paying the bills for hand surgery on the Hubs. The year before he'd accidentally fallen down the stairs in a vacant house he was showing to potential buyers and broke his finger in multiple places, requiring surgery and pins. (I swear, I had nothing to do with his fall. I was not even in the house when it happened.)

The Hubs held up his permanently crooked finger. "Now we match," he said.

"Aww," I said, snottily.

The Hubs got serious. "Does it hurt a lot? Do you think it's broken?"

"No, I don't think it's broken. I think it's badly sprained."

"Okay, well, there's nothing a doctor can do about that except charge us a hundred bucks to tell you it's sprained."

"Fine. If it feels worse, I'll go and see him."

"Good idea."

The finger stopped hurting, but it never went back to its original position. It leaned to the right and couldn't bend properly, but the Hubs was right. It was my most useless finger and so I barely noticed it until a year after when I went for my annual check up and my doctor asked about it.

"What happened to your pinky, Jen?" he asked, looking closely at my hand.

"Oh, uhhh ..." I stammered. I didn't really want to tell my doctor that my husband and I were wrestling like two fools and I fell and hurt it. So I said, "I'm not sure."

"You're not sure? An injury like that wouldn't go unnoticed. You must remember hurting it."

I stalled some more. "Umm ..."

"It looks like the ligament was torn and then didn't heal properly. Did you get medical help when it first happened?"

"No," I admitted. "Can it be fixed now?"

He shook his head. "No, it can't. Not unless you want to go through surgery and rehab."

"Looks like my hand modeling days are over," I joked.

The doctor looked at me very seriously. "Jen, this is no laughing matter. This was a serious injury and you didn't get treatment for it. Why?"

"It wasn't a big deal."

Now the doctor took a closer look at me. "Is your eye purple? Is it bruised?"

I quickly covered my left eye with my left hand—the one with the fucked up pinky. "Yeah," I said.

"What happened there?" He pulled out a light and touched my bruise lightly.

"The baby kicked me in the face yesterday when I was changing his diaper," I said, laughing. Gomer hated getting his diaper changed and sometimes he could get me good if I wasn't fast enough to dodge his kicks.

The doctor didn't laugh. Instead he sighed heavily and sat back in his chair. "Okay, Jen. I want you to stay here for a minute. There's someone I want you to meet."

He left me alone in the office for a few minutes and then a woman came in and sat down.

"Hi," she said. "I'm the counselor here in the office and I thought it would be a good idea if we had a little chat."

I squirmed in my seat. What the hell? Did he think I was depressed or something? Why did he send in the counselor?

"Do you want to tell me what's going on at home, Jen?" she asked, kindly. "It's all confidential. We won't tell your husband."

OH SHIT.

Finally, the lightbulb went on in my dim brain. "You think my husband abuses me?"

She shrugged. "You tell me. Your pinky, your eye, the fact that you don't want to seek medical treatment for your injuries."

"Oh. My. God," I said.

"I know," she said. "It's okay. Go ahead."

"No! You don't understand! My husband doesn't abuse me. The baby really did kick me in the eye yesterday. He does it all the time, because I'm slow as shit. And my husband ... we ... we just mess around together and I get hurt."

"Mess around?"

"Yeah, we goof off."

"You get hurt a lot?" she asked, concerned.

"I don't know. Every now and again." Fuck, I wasn't making it any better!

"Why don't you get treatment when you get hurt from *messing around* with your husband?"

I stayed silent at that point. I didn't feel like telling this woman that my husband and I were self-employed and had shitty health insurance and had to have full-on pros and cons discussions before going to see a doctor. If there was no blood and you were still conscious, then the visit was up for discussion. We had a baby now and he had to see the doctor all the time, so our money went to his ridiculously high co-pays. I could live with a crooked finger or a black eye, but my baby needed his vaccinations.

I appreciated that this woman thought she was trying to help me and I loved that she wasn't letting anything go, but my problem wasn't my husband abusing me. My problem was that I needed more affordable health care. She wasn't going to change that and I wasn't going to convince her that my husband wasn't beating me.

I shrugged. "Can I go now?" I asked.

"Of course," she said. "No one is stopping you."

"Great," I said, picking up my stuff. "Thanks."

"Are you okay to drive?" she asked.

"I didn't drive. My husband and baby are in the waiting room."

"I see," she said. "I'll walk you out."

She walked me to the waiting room and gave the Hubs a scathing once over. The Hubs was oblivious.

"Here, I want to give you these," she said, handing me some brochures. "Please read them."

"Thanks," I mumbled, taking the brochures and shoving them in my diaper bag.

We left the doctor's office and got on the elevator. "What're the brochures for?" the Hubs asked me.

"Take a look." I pulled them out and handed them to him.

"Are you being abused? Know your legal rights," the Hubs read. "The national domestic hotline number. What the hell?"

I held up my mangled pinky. "I just had a full-on intervention in there."

The Hubs laughed. "Little do they know *I'm* the abused party in this relationship!"

I laughed too. "Right? Well, now I need a new doctor. Because when Gomer kicks me so hard he breaks my jaw, they're never going to believe me."

"I'm not sure a broken jaw is worth a doctor's visit. I mean, what can they really do for that?" the Hubs said.

I punched him in the arm.

"Ow. Careful, or you'll hurt your other hand," the Hubs teased.

I stopped hitting him, because he was absolutely right.

CHAPTER 16

THIRD COUSINS CAN TOTALLY MARRY IN SOME STATES

ON THE FIRST day of my freshman year in college I met my dad's old girlfriend who I did not even know existed.

Let me explain. I attended a very small private college. It is a family tradition to attend this college. We're like the Bush legacy at Yale or the Kennedy clan at Harvard. Only we're the Manns and instead of Yale or Harvard the college we attended was like a fairly decent community college in the middle of nowhere. It wasn't just my parents who attended this college. Several of my aunts and uncles met there and many of my cousins met their spouses there, too.

My family is not the only one to instill this sense of tradition in their offspring. There are many "old" families at this particular college and after awhile it started to feel like you might be related to every guy you wanted to date—because you probably were.

In fact, when my brother, C.B., was a freshman, he told me he had an upcoming date with a young lady. He gave me her name and I said, "I'm pretty sure she's our third cousin."

"You're kidding!" he groaned.

"Nope. She's from Canada, right? And her last name is MacMillan?"

"Yes."

"Yeah, I'm pretty sure we met her at a family reunion several years ago. Her grandma is Alice. And Alice is Grandma's younger sister. That's a fairly close branch on the family tree, don't you think?"

"Oh my God! I think I remember her now! Eww. Shit, why are we related to all the hot girls?" my brother lamented.

I don't think it was any surprise when neither C.B. nor myself married anyone we met at college. When you have a mother with fifty first cousins who then turn around and send their kids to a college of eleven hundred kids, the dating pool is a bit too cloudy at that point. It felt downright incestuous.

However, cousins were the least of my concern when I stepped on campus. I didn't even know yet how murky the dating pool was because I was too busy dodging friends of my parents. Many of my parents' friends had grown up and decided to never leave college life. They all signed up to teach. When my Dad looked at my schedule he was like, "Look, Eloise, she has Harrington! Remember him?"

"I'm not surprised. I saw his wife in the book store. Apparently, she's the manager!" Mom said.

"Looks like Kline is here too. He's teaching business. I'd love to stop by and say hi," Dad said. "I haven't seen him in twenty years."

After my parents helped me unpack my books, hang up my frilly curtains, make my bed, and fold my clothes, they went out to find their old school chums. "Want to go come, Jenni?" Dad asked. "Might be good for you to kiss up a bit before classes start."

"Pass," I said.

I'd already seen a few people that my parents knew and it was super uncomfortable. Everyone stared at me like I was some kind of mutant. It had nothing to do with my terrible perm and everything to do with the age on my student I.D. Since my parents were so young when I was born, I was one of the first of their generation's offspring to show up on campus. The forty-something-year-old faculty and staff were not thrilled to see me, because I was like a harbinger of death to them. I reminded them instantly that they were no longer young and cool. Nothing killed their buzz faster than realizing they were old enough to have a child who was a college student.

That first morning I woke up late (of course I did—I'm always late) and I had to run to my first class. I was a bit out of breath from running across campus. The building was a little farther than I had calculated the night before and an eight o'clock class came a little earlier than I anticipated. It didn't help that my mom wasn't there to make sure I was out of bed after messing around with my new friends in the dorm until two in the morning. I finally found the building and ran up the stairs. I figured I could just slide into a seat in the back of the room and hopefully catch a nap, but when I arrived I saw that I was one of only about twelve people who were taking the class. *Darn you, small and intimate classes!* I thought. *It sounded good in the marketing brochure, but there was no way to sneak in late!* The students were arranged in a semi-circle in front of the chalkboard and a woman closely resembling Stevie Nicks was standing in front of the board introducing herself.

"Well, hello! Come in!" she called as I tried to slip in unnoticed. "Pull up a chair and join our group."

I grabbed a chair and sat down.

She said, "As I was saying, my classroom is very informal and so please call me Lucinda. This semester we will be spending a great deal of time together and I think it's important to know one another well, so I'd like to go around the room and have you introduce yourself to the group and tell us a bit about your background. Let us know *who* you are. Don't be afraid to drop the veil and let us in. What makes you tick? Why don't we start with the young lady who was late?" She looked at me.

I took a deep breath. Twenty years later I have absolutely no trouble speaking in front of a group, in fact, I like it, but at eighteen I was a basket of nerves. Even though there were only twelve faces peering at me—well, thirteen if you counted Lucinda—it felt like a hundred. I thought about Lucinda's questions. Drop the veil? I wasn't even sure what she meant by that. I finally went for it, "Uhh...okay. I'm Jenni Mann—errr..." Damn it!! I couldn't believe it. I blew my first chance! You see, before I left for college I decided that I was going to reinvent myself. I was tired of quiet, meek Jenni with an adorable "i" who let everyone walk all over her and never stood up for herself. Going forward, I was going to be *Jen*. Jen was strong and confident and cool-ish (strong and confident were probably doable, but cool would take some work). I corrected myself, "I mean, I'm *Jen* Mann. I'm from—"

"Wait. I'm sorry," Lucinda interrupted. "But did you just say your name is Jenni Mann?"

I frowned. "Yes, but it's Jen, actually. I go by Jen," I said.

Lucinda waved a hand at me. "Okay, yes, fine, Jen. But Jen *Mann*?

"Yes."

"No. It can't be. Surely you're not old enough," she sort of mumbled to herself. "Impossible."

I thought maybe she was crazy. I looked at the other students to see if they had noticed her odd behavior. No one appeared at all interested. "Excuse me?" I asked.

"I'm sorry, it's just that I used to know a Jeffrey Mann and for a moment I thought maybe you were related ... somehow."

"Yes, I'm related to Jeffrey."

"You are? Are you his ... niece, or ..."

"I'm his daughter."

She choked. "Jeffrey Mann is your dad?" she asked, her eyes widened.

"Yes."

"How can that be? Are you eighteen?"

"Of course," I said, highly offended. Duh. Did she think I was some kind of twelve-year-old prodigy? I looked young, but not that young!

"No," she shook her head. "It must be a different Jeffrey Mann. The one I'm thinking of is far too young to have an eighteen-year-old. He's my age and I only have a six-year-old, for goodness sake!" (Looking back, I'd like to formally apologize to Lucinda for being so judgmental at this point in the conversation. I know I rolled my eyes dramatically and thought, "Get over yourself, lady. Face it: you're *old*!" Because now that I've hit my forties and, I too, have small children, I am horrified by my friends who are posting high school graduation pictures on Facebook. I am also in complete denial that I am old enough to have a child anywhere near college-age. I get it now. I didn't then. It wasn't Lucinda's fault that my parents decided to get married and have a baby all before my mother turned twenty-one. Also, my mother would like me to make it clear to you, dear reader, that she didn't HAVE to get married. She WANTED to get married. There's a difference. Sure, they were young, but they were in love, etc., etc.)

I shrugged. "Okay. If you say so. Anyway, I'm Jen. I'm from—"

"Wait. Did your father attend college here?" Lucinda asked, interrupting me again.

I sighed. It was getting ridiculous. "Yes."

"He graduated from here?" she asked.

I sighed again. "Yes. He and my mother both did."

"Who is your mother?" Lucinda asked.

"Eloise Mann."

"No, what was her maiden name?" Lucinda asked, exasperated. As if I were the one holding up the other introductions with all of the super invasive and probing questions!

"Shepherd," I said.

"Hmm ... yes, it must be a different Jeffrey Mann, because I don't remember Eloise Shepherd."

"Okay. Anyway, I'm from—"

"Your dad is about this tall," Lucinda raised her arm, "and has dark hair and green eyes?"

That was when I started getting creeped out. Plus, people hadn't been paying us any attention before, but now all eyes were on us. I gulped. "Yes. Except, he's kind of gray now."

"Sure. That makes sense," Lucinda said. She furrowed her brow. "Eloise Shepherd! I remember her now! She was a senior my freshman year. She was much older than me. That's why I don't know her."

"I'm not sure. Depends how old you are. Are you my dad's age?"

"Yes, Jeffrey and I were freshmen together," Lucinda said, smiling.

"Weird, because my mom is a year younger than my dad."

"Impossible!" she practically howled.

Finally, a busybody spoke up, "Lucinda, we're learning so much about you! The veil is really coming down! This is so interesting. Can you tell us how you knew Jenni's dad?"

I glared at her and sent her a telepathic message: *Thanks, asshole.*

Lucinda looked around and it was like she finally realized we were not alone and that she looked a teensy bit like a crazy person. She smoothed her peasant skirt over her hips and said, "Of course. It's not a secret and I'm not ashamed to share. I used to date Jen's dad, Jeffrey." There was an audible gasp in the room and I think mine was the loudest.

Let me be clear: of course I knew my dad dated other women before he met my mom, but I never once thought that someday his ex might be my college professor. *EWWWWWWW!*

She went on. "We were quite ... close. He always called me LuLu."

"Were you guys serious?" the busybody inquired.

I looked around for a window to jump out of.

"We really enjoyed being together, but we had a very volatile relationship. It was quite explosive sometimes."

"Psst," the guy next to me whispered. "I think your dad totally boned her."

I wanted to kick him until he was dead. *Shut. The. Fuck. Up.*

"We were going to be professors together. Is he a professor, Jen?"

"No. He never got his Ph.D. He's a business executive."

"Well, that must be your mother's influence on him.

When we dated we dreamed of a life in academia. He had a brilliant mind. It's a shame he's wasting it on business."

"Were you in love?" the busybody asked.

I'm not listening, I thought. I prayed for a giant meteor to hit the building.

I didn't know what Lucinda was going to say but I couldn't let her answer.

I yelled, "As I was saying, I'm Jen. I'm from—"

"The next time you talk to your dad, please let him know that LuLu says hello," Lucinda said with a little giggle.

I nodded silently.

"Now, I think we've learned plenty about Jen," Lucinda said. "Who's next?"

━━━

That night my parents called to check in to see how my first day of college went. I was curled in my bed reliving the nightmare of my encounter with Lucinda.

"Sooo," my mother started. "did you meet anyone interesting today?" (I didn't know it yet, but this would be an ongoing theme for the next four years. My mom and dad felt like college was *the place* to find a good husband. I'm pretty sure the brochure said, "Ring by spring or your money back!")

"I sure did! Is Dad there?"

"I'm on the line too," Dad said.

"Oh good. I have a message for you: LuLu sends her regards," I sneered.

There was dead silence. Finally my mom asked, "Who?"

"Yeah, who?" Dad asked.

"LuLu," I said. "You know, Dad, your old flame who is now *my professor*! The woman who spent half of today's class telling everyone what a hot stud you were in college and how mom must be at least ten years older than you because there is no way *you're* old enough to have a kid in college, because then *she'd* be old enough to have a kid in college! I think she hoped I was Mom's from a previous relationship or some kind of little kid genius."

"Wait. Who?" Dad asked. "LuLu? Jenni, I have no clue who you are talking about."

"Dr. Lucinda Parker. She's some kind new age hippie type. Totally stuck in the sixties."

"Everyone was a hippie when we were in college," Dad said, exasperated. "I think she's got the wrong guy."

"It sure didn't sound like it. Why don't you ask my entire class? They were literally enraptured! She went on and on about your dreamy green eyes and your fiery relationship. She used the word 'volatile'! It was positively revolting."

Dad laughed nervously.

"LuLu Parker! Now, I know who she is!" Mom said. "I met her the first night I arrived on campus. She was a sophomore and she was a hippie type! She sort of looked like Stevie Nicks."

"Ding! Ding! Ding!" I said. "That's the one—she still does."

"Yes, I remember her. Hang on, you guys were dating, Jeff?" she asked my dad. "That's weird, because I could swear she's the one who introduced us as at *the mixer* that night. Jen, you do know your dad and I met the first night of my freshman year, right?"

"Yes, Mom. I know," I sighed. "At the mixer."

"Is there a mixer tonight?" she asked, hopefully.

"I don't think they do that stuff anymore. That's really old-fashioned."

"Do you remember, Jeff?"

"Of course, I remember."

"He was trying to be cool and he ended up looking like a dork because he spilled a soda all over me. And then I could swear it was LuLu who said, 'Eloise meet Jeff.' I'm sure she was there."

"Yeah, because it was probably LuLu's soda he spilled on you," I said.

"No, I don't think so," Mom said.

"Why would she lie?" I asked. "She knew I would tell you guys."

"It was so cute," Mom continued.

"Hilarious," Dad agreed.

"Dad! Did you or did you not date LuLu?" I asked.

Dad replied, "I don't remember anyone before your mom. I've forgotten them all."

"Once he fell head over heels with that soda, he fell head over heels for me," Mom said.

Yup. My parents met just like a bad rom-com. My mom was the quiet, reserved Preacher's daughter enjoying her first night away from home and my dad was the crass, loud dude who was showing off and accidentally spilled a drink all over her. As the cold liquid soaked them both, they locked eyes and realized there was no one else in the world. She stole his heart and he changed his wilding (and apparently, hippie-loving) ways to be with her and they've never looked back.

Every time I heard that story growing up I wasn't sure if I should be impressed or worried. On one had, it's an adorable story full of mischief and love at first sight, but on the hand, that is one tough act to follow. Holy shit. No pressure, Jen, but just go to the same college we went to, attend the mixer on the first night and wait for the stars to align so you can meet your future husband in some ridiculous over the top sitcom way so you'll have your own adorable story to tell for the rest of your life.

"Hey, Jen!" my room mate called walking into the room. "Hang up that phone! It's time for the mixer!"

"I knew it!" Mom cried. "It's mixer night, Jeff!"

"Is that the best your hair does?" my room mate asked. "I've got a guy I want you to meet!"

"Try combing it, Jenni!" Mom said. "You might meet your future husband tonight. You can't meet him with bad hair!"

"My hair has a mind of its own. It does what it wants," I said.

My room mate shrugged. "It will be fine, I guess."

"All right, Mom," I said. "I gotta go. I guess I'm going to the mixer."

"Of course you are! Good luck!" Mom trilled. "Oh, and, Jenni, please tell LuLu thank you *so much* for introducing me to her boyfriend!"

It was probably a good thing my hair did not "do any better" because the guy my room mate introduced me to that night was my cousin.

CHAPTER 17

GOMER'S BEAUTIFUL BIRTH STORY

(ALTERNATE TITLE: WELL, AT LEAST I DIDN'T SHIT MYSELF)

I DON'T KNOW what it is about women (myself includ-ed), but we looooove to tell our birth stories. Everyone has a good one, don't they? One woman I know had a marathon pushing session only to end up in an O.R. with an emer-gency C-section. Another had such a horrific episiotomy that her doctor couldn't make heads or tails out of her hooha (literally) and botched her stitch-up so badly it had to be redone at her six week check up. She calls that the six weeks she had two vaginas. Another got such a kick ass epidural she sat up and played gin while she labored. At the opposite end is my friend who silently (and drug free, of course) welcomed her child into the world in a bath tub (or is a birth tub?) in her living room surrounded by her closest friends, family, doulas, midwives, neighbors, yogi, astrologer, and pizza delivery guy (Okay, I exaggerated. The pizza delivery guy wasn't invited, because she'd *never* eat take out pizza, but you get my drift). What I'm trying to say is, we've all got a story and our birth story is so unique to us that we feel the need to share it with anyone who has a good thirty minutes and doesn't mind looking at cell phone pictures of slimy, wrinkly, old-man-looking babies and ... oh, my God, is that a tuft *pubic hair* in the corner of that one photo??

Well, get comfortable, because I'm going to tell you one of my birth stories. I'll tell you about Gomer's birth. (Relax, Adolpha, I'm not telling Gomer's story because he's my favorite, he was literally born first, so it just makes sense to start with him.)

It was a cold and stormy night in 2004 and the Hubs and I were home alone (Ahh...remember those days, Hubs??) watching *Survivor* (I have a good memory) when I noticed that I'd been ignoring a steady run of contractions for about an hour. I wasn't due for another month and I just wasn't paying too close attention yet. (This is sort of my M.O. Let's not forget, I was actually pregnant with this same kid for twelve weeks and ignored *all* the symptoms and instead opted to believe I might have a brain tumor. Pregnancy was a little out of my comfort zone, ya think?)

After an hour of this, I finally sat up—literally. My fat ass had been lounging on the couch all night at that point. I sat up and mentioned my discomfort to the Hubs. Like the couple of tools that we are, we finally cracked the spine on our copy of the blasted *What to Expect When You're Expecting*. (Thank you to my sister-in-law Ida who had the common sense to give us this book early on, probably thinking I might actually read it *before* I went into labor. Yeah, whoops on that. I didn't really read much of it except for the chapter about pregnant women who were compelled to eat dirt. *What the what??* Does anyone really know anyone who did this?) Anyhoo, back to my story. Thanks to the ever helpful and knowledgeable writer of *WTEWYE* we determined I MIGHT be in pre-term labor OR it COULD just be Braxton-Hicks OR there was a CHANCE it could be false labor. The author indicated that a pregnant woman shouldn't worry, because a mother will simply "know" if she's in labor. You know what? Very fucking unhelpful! I didn't *know*. That's why I was reading the stupid book! I think this book must have been written by a lawyer, because there was so much ass-covering going on I couldn't diagnose shit. Truly. If you were trying to diagnose shit, the author probably would have said, "It MIGHT be feces, it COULD be mud, but there is a CHANCE it's chocolate. Find a pregnant lady who eats dirt and ask her to try it, she'll just *know*."

We figured, that between the Hubs and I, the two of us had watched enough *Dr. Quinn Medicine Woman* that we knew we should at least time the contractions. We got out a watch and kept track of the contractions for the next hour or so and found a pattern: four to five minutes apart. Oh shit, that was water boiling time! Since we could barely understand if I was in labor, we knew we weren't going to be able to birth this baby in the family room—and we didn't have a care about medical bills thanks to our fabulous insurance in those heady pre-self-employed days—we high-tailed it to the emergency room for a professional to do the job.

At this point, it's important to note that it was close to midnight and we were going to the ER with nothing packed. I was sure that our baby was going to enter the world in a matter of mere minutes and the hell that was going to happen on my bedroom floor while I searched for my cutest pjs! Surely, you didn't think I had a bag packed already? It was a month before my baby was due. Packing a bag that early? That's plain crazy. Plus, I don't have that many pjs. I can't take a good set out of the rotation for a whole month! So, I can get away with my excuse for why I didn't have a bag packed, but I really can't forgive myself for not grabbing the camera. Yup. Name two assholes who went to the hospital to have a baby (before good cell phone cameras) and didn't bring the camera? Answer: Jen and the Hubs.

The Hubs dropped me off at the door (mostly because the car was brand spanking new and amniotic fluid kills resale value) and I waddled in. Our local hospitals are used to catering to the crazy pregnant ladies. The crazy pregnant ladies keep the lights on and pay the bills, but even then, there were many employees who looked a little surprised when I bustled in demanding a bed. The nurse looked at me like I was a simpleton when I told her what was going on.

"I'm having contractions! They're four minutes apart. I'm going to have a baby!" I told her.

"Okay, okay, settle down. Are your contractions strong?"

"Strong?"

"Are they painful?"

"Oh. Yeah. A little. I mean, like a twinge."

"A twinge?"

"Yeah, like gas."

"Your contractions feel like gas pains?"

"Yeah, they're just a little uncomfortable."

"I see. Okay, honey. I'm going to help you out. Come with me." She hooked me up to the monitors all the while telling me, "You first time moms are so cute. You always think you're in labor."

"Well, the book said ..."

"Yes, yes, I know what the book says." She rolled her eyes. "It also says it could be Braxton-Hicks or false labor. You know, honey, you could feel this way for the next month and a half."

"No! My due date is only a month away now. I'm having the baby in a month. My time will be up in one month," I said like Rain Man ranting about one minute to Wapner.

"Well, your forty weeks will be up in less than a month, but many first timers go late. You might still have a good six weeks left, honey. Let's just see what the baby thinks is going on. He knows the most. He's the one in charge."

After an hour without an increase in the intensity of my contractions, she decided to send us home.

"False labor!" the nurse declared as she started stripping the sheets off my bed.

"But I'm dilated!" I argued.

"You're a one. You can walk around for weeks dilated at a one," she said. "Go on home. Get some rest. You're going to need it."

I was in the bathroom getting dressed and feeling incredibly stupid while the Hubs was in the other room speaking to the nurse. I heard him say, "You must hate all of us new parents who come here in false labor."

She chuckled and said, "Nah, that's not so bad. What's worse is when they come back *again* that same day insisting they're in labor. *That's* when it gets annoying."

We went home. By then it was the middle of the night and we were exhausted and we needed to go to bed.

That's when my water broke.

At least I *think* that's what happened.

Again, it was *really* unclear in the damn book. I was told a GUSH. My friends who have had their water break have described entire minivans totaled out by the water damage (thus, the Hubs shooing me out of the new car ASAP) or kitchen floors that warped. I was expecting a waterfall-type situation. I imagined roaring rapids. Not: *Gee, I need to use the bathroom. Hmm...I sure am peeing a lot. Well, they did fill me with lots of fluids, but this is sort of ridiculous. Still peeing. What's going on? Oh fuck it, I'm tired. I'm going to bed.*

Honestly, I was too exhausted to think about it and the nurse's words kept coming back to haunt me. I did *not* want to be that uber-crazy pregnant lady who went to the hospital with false labor *twice*.

So, I crawled into bed, figuring I was too tired and ashamed to go back to the hospital at that point and that if it truly was labor the pains would wake me up. (Yes, I'm an idiot. But I think we established that long ago. Look, nothing gets between me and my beauty sleep. I think deep down Gomer knew I needed that one last night of deep sleep, because I wasn't going to get another one for at least four more years and so he chilled out all night and let me rest.)

I woke up at about six o'clock the next morning feeling *very* uncomfortable. Those pains were not similar to gas. Finally, the book was right. I *knew* this time it was for real.

I started making calls. I called my doctor first and he was already aware I'd been to the hospital the night before (word gets around!) and I think he wanted to save me the embarrassment of being sent home twice, so he suggested we meet at his office instead so she could check me first.

Next, I called my mother and told her it was time. She probably screamed. I don't really remember that part, just the part where I was watching *Survivor*. Go figure. The mind is a tricky thing.

Then I called my Aunt Ruby. Aunt Ruby had been a labor and delivery nurse for years and I'd asked her to be in the delivery room with me as my back up. That way, if things went sideways and need be, she could take over. If Gomer was in danger, I wanted Aunt Ruby to slap on some gloves and yell, "Clear the room! I've got this!" or "Stop farking around [Aunt Ruby would never say "fucking"] and get this girl to an O.R.! To hell with her birth plan, let's just get this baby out!"

I met my doctor at his office and he checked me and told me that sure enough my water had broken (yeah, that wasn't all pee—but in my defense it also was not a gush) and I was in labor. He said, "Today's the day!"

I wasn't ready.

My bag still wasn't packed. I didn't have relaxing music to play when my baby entered the world. I didn't have a scented candle to neutralize the antiseptic hospital smell. I didn't have *ah-dor-able* pjs to wear. I didn't have essential oils to rub on my nether regions so I wouldn't rip from hole to hole. Eh, who am I kidding? I was never going to have any of that shit, I didn't even have my hair combed, let alone a damn birth plan.

"Well, at least you're here," I said gratefully to my doctor. "We can do this together."

"Yeah, about that. I have a family thing today, so I won't be there for the delivery, but I want you to meet someone." He stepped out in the hallway and brought in a woman in scrubs.

"This is Hillary. She's one of our midwives and she's going to take care of you."

"Midwife? But I signed up for a doctor. No offense, Hillary."

"None taken." She said, clearly offended. *Super.*

"Jen, we talked about this. We have many doctors and midwives in our practice and there is always a chance that you would get someone other than your primary provider."

"Uh huh," I said skeptically. "But what do you have going on today?" I mean, honestly, what was he doing that day? It was the middle of the week. Who has a "family thing" in the middle of the week at seven in the morning?

"Did you know that many of our patients actually prefer to have the midwife at their birth? They are able to provide you with a lot more attention than a doctor can."

"How come?" I asked, warming up to the idea of more attention, because I can be a bit of an attention whore sometimes. (Okay, all the time.)

"Well, they have fewer patients to see and they won't be called out for emergency surgeries, so they have more free time to spend with you and help you labor. They also have lots of non-invasive ways to help you deliver. Most of them have had a baby or two, so they know exactly what you're feeling. Hillary will be great for you."

"Huh. Okay." I mean, really, what was my choice? What was I going to say? My water had broken, I was in labor, I was a complete moron, and I needed someone to get this baby out of me! Aunt Ruby was really just a back up plan, I couldn't rely on her to get the deed done. I also couldn't throw a fit and demand my doctor stay. That was never going to work. I'd already pissed off Hillary a bit and now I needed to make sure she liked me so she'd do a good job delivering my baby. "I mean, sounds great!" I said enthusiastically.

We went to the hospital and they admitted me while the Hubs went home to throw my rattiest jammies ("How am I supposed to know which jammies were the new ones you bought for the hospital? They all look the same to me," the Hubs would whine to me several weeks later when I finally got around to looking at the pictures of me in my tattered pjs. "You should have packed a bag before we left!") and my toothbrush in a plastic bag and grab the camera. When I met my new nurse I said, "Hi. Yeah, could you please tell that nurse, Janice, from last night that I was totally right? I *am* having a baby today. That chick didn't have a clue what she was talking about. 'Kay, thanks, bye."

My new nurse was a total see you next Tuesday. In her defense, my treatment of Nurse Janice probably didn't help, but I always wonder about people like this. Teachers who don't like children, doctors who don't want to touch a sick person, and labor and delivery nurses who don't like first time mothers. With her personality she should be in the O.R. where her patient is unconscious. She sneered at me as if somehow I had fooled everyone into thinking that I was in labor just so I could show up Nurse Janice.

She also wasn't thrilled with my "support team."

I had the Hubs who had been warned within an inch of his life that I would only allow him in the room if he gave me positive support. I'd heard horror stories of friends and acquaintances whose husbands told them "C'mon you wimp, you can push harder than that. Put your back into it!" We had gone over a list of acceptable, encouraging phrases he could use. (I might not have packed a bag or written a birth plan or brushed my hair, but I *had* coached the Hubs. I had my priorities straight!) I had suggested he could add his own ideas to the mix, but instead, he just chose to stick to the script I'd given him. So, for the entire 14 hours of labor and delivery I heard this: "You're doing great...I'm so proud of you...I love you...Have an ice chip." Pop an ice chip down my gullet and repeat. It drove everyone in the room bananas. I didn't care. It was my own fault. I knew he was a literal person when I married him and I love that he did exactly what I asked of him (even if he almost choked me to death with ice chips).

I had my mother who I promptly put on notice that she needed to keep her cold fucking hands to herself. What the hell, woman?? They were ice cold and she kept touching me. It was pissing me off and I knew it was going to be a long day if she didn't keep her hands in her pockets.

Aunt Ruby was there, keeping a close eye on Nurse Bitch and ready to jump in if the shit hit the fan.

Ida was supposed to be the final member of my team, but my brother had selfishly scheduled elective gallbladder surgery that day without any consideration that I *might* go into labor. I swear, it was like he cared more about that gallbladder and the grief it was causing him than the rest of us. He should have scheduled it for a month after my due date so there couldn't possibly be any interference.

Our joint medical needs actually caused a lot of problems for Ida, because she had her own newborn to take care of and a husband in surgery and my mom was completely unavailable to help, because she was at my bedside touching me with her icicle hands. Ida got stuck with my dad, who went to sit at my brother's hospital with her. (Yeah, the jerk didn't even schedule his surgery at the hospital where I was delivering. Something about it wasn't in his insurance plan or something. Whatever, C.B.!) When I say my dad "sat" at the hospital with her, that's being generous. My dad and I have the same coping mechanism for stress. When we are put into potentially stressful situations we sleep. So my dad was with Ida, but he was probably stretched out on the floor in some dark, quiet waiting room catching some zzz's. So, in all actuality, Ida was alone dealing with her newborn and C.B.'s surgery.

I started out that day feeling pretty good because my contractions were still fairly light. I was in a bit of a panic, though, because I thought I still had a month to go so I had scheduled two closings and two clients were supposed to write contracts on homes all on that day. (Yes, I see the hypocrisy in my scheduling closings and then being mad at

C.B. for scheduling his surgery, but I just like to give C.B. grief. It lets him know that I care.) I sat in my hospital bed hooked up to monitors with my files spread out around me while I made calls to get shit sorted. (I was Super Woman in those days. It was easy. I didn't have kids yet.) The Hubs didn't work with me at that point, so I had to find help elsewhere. I managed to get a colleague to write up the two contracts with me on the speaker phone with my clients. One of these two people really didn't like being handed off to another agent. She actually had the nerve to bitch to me that I was unprofessional for going into labor and she really would prefer that I not write her contract over the phone and that we should be doing it in person. *Yeahhh...I'm sorry, I can't be there, but I'm having a baby today, psycho!* (This became a recurring theme with people in my life who have never had a baby. If you haven't had one, let me give you a tip—they're kind of a big deal and you really need to give it 100% of your attention.)

I kept telling Nurse Bitch that my contractions were getting stronger, but the machines weren't picking them up so she didn't believe me, because apparently, I got off on lying about contractions. Instead she just kept upping my dosage of Pitocin. Pretty soon it was time to get my epidural. This was a disaster. The doctor arrived with a wing man. I was introduced to the wing man and told that he was a student who would be watching the procedure while the pro actually did the work. I think it would have gone better if we'd given the student a crack at it. I think my doctor had performance anxiety. *WTF, doc?? Just get it in there!!* After a couple of tries, the metric shit ton of Pitocin that Nurse Bitch had loaded me with kicked in all at once. The contractions were so fucking fierce and I was twitching so much, I about got a needle in my neck. Apparently, that was what the anesthesiologist was waiting for. He rose to the challenge of trying to pin the proverbial tail on the ass and *finally* got the line where it needed to be and the medicine started flowing. Almost immediately the right side of my body went numb. The left side...not so much. The Pitocin was doing its job and my contractions were raging over the right half my body. I was miserable. *Thanks, Dr. Douchebag, please send me your outrageous bill and I'll only pay half since only half my body is numb.*

Needless to say, the files and phone went away and I got down to the real business at hand. There was no more Super Woman. She died that day. (I'm not sure she'll ever be back.) After many more hours of being curled into the fetal position while a war was fought in my motherfucking uterus —I mean, some slight discomfort—it was time to push. Hallelujah!

I don't remember much about pushing, except it was painful (on one side) and I did it for a long time.

Like hours.

"You're doing great...I'm so proud of you...I love you... Have an ice chip...You're doing great...I'm so proud of you...I love you...Have an ice chip...You're doing—"

Then! Suddenly, he was interrupted by a flurry of activity in the room. Lots of nurses running around. I started panicking and I looked for Aunt Ruby. She was down at the far end holding a leg. I said, "What's going on? What are these people doing here, Aunt Ruby?"

Hillary smiled at me and said, "We're having a birthday party!"

"Oh no you're not! Get the hell out of my room! Go have your party somewhere else!" I yelled.

"Jen, your baby is coming. The birthday party is for *him*!"

Whoops. Yeah, I thought random hospital staff were going to have a birthday party in my labor and delivery room. Don't judge me, people, I was a fucking mess. I'd been pushing for hours. I had broken blood vessels all over my face from exerting myself and a permanently dilated pupil that would require a visit with a neurosurgeon. I was so hot. I kept tearing off my clothes and I was begging my mother to put her frigid hands on my bare breasts to cool me down. My body was so completely numb on one side, I was worried that I might *never* get feeling back again and oh yeah, I was starving. It was nine in the evening and I hadn't had anything except encouraging ice chips since my dinner of oatmeal the night before. (Scary good memory, right? Don't ask me what year the Magna Carta was signed though. T.V. and food, those are the only areas in my memory bank.) So, yes, I was a bit delusional and it did not seem at all abnormal to me for the hospital staff to throw a birthday party in my room for one of their colleagues.

"One more push and he'll be out!" cried Hillary.

You know how a lot of people have beautiful birthing stories of the baby coming into the world to the gentle sounds of the rainforest in a dimly lit room surrounded by special people and loved ones? How the mother looked into the father's eyes on that final push so they could feel that everlasting bond of love that ties them together with this little person that they've created together?

Yeah, fuck that shit. That did *not* happen to me. My most vivid memory of the final push that delivered my son was me thinking, "This is fucking *it*! I don't have anything left. I'm going to die!" As he exited my body I looked up at all the people at the foot of the bed, trying one last time for that everlasting bond of love moment thing. There was Hillary looking all Zen and communing with Mother

Nature, Nurse Bitch glaring at the clock because she was fucking *done*, a couple of extra nurses I'd never seen before, Aunt Ruby sweating a little from hoisting my leg for so long, and my mom ugly crying. I couldn't see the Hubs. Earlier he'd taken a quick peek downtown and then decided he was of better use gagging me on ice chips than watching me squeeze a bowling ball out of my nether regions. I remember a few more random people, but the one who stands out the most in my mind was the wing man—the student anesthesiologist—standing head and shoulders above everyone else with a huge shit-eating grin on his face staring at the miracle of life transpiring in my wide open hooha and giving me two thumbs up. I felt pure rage enter my body. I wanted to scream, "Are you fucking kidding me?? *This* is my everlasting bond of love? *This* is the last thing I see before I hear my sweet baby's cry? This doofus checking out my lady parts?" But I didn't, because by that point, I'd had it. I was done. Someone needed to stick a fork in me. I would not have argued if an actual three-ring circus had set up shop at the end of my bed. I took one last look at the goofy student and thought, *Oh fuck it, at least he gave me two thumbs up.*

CHAPTER 18

IS IT TOO HARSH TO SAY I HOPE THIS ONE DIES ALONE?

WHEN I WAS a junior in high school I had a mean crush on a boy named Joey. Actually, I had crushes on several boys, but Joey was my favorite. He was super smart *and* easy on the eyes—a double whammy. He was tall and athletic and had the cutest dimples when he smiled. Now, a lot of times when someone tells you a story about a boy she longed for, this is the part where she tells you the boy of her dreams didn't even know she existed. Well, don't worry, I didn't have that problem. Joey knew who I was. He knew me well. In fact, Joey liked me. A lot. But not *a lot-a lot* if you know what I mean. That was because I was—and always have been—the girl with the good personality.

I was the homely girl who could make you laugh with my biting wit. I was the girl who was down for doing goofy shit because I didn't worry about how my hair looked while I was doing that goofy shit. I was also the girl who was easy to talk to. Probably too easy to talk to. Joey would spend hours—nay, days—talking to me about all the other girls he was pining for.

I was the one who sat silently by his side while he broke

down what Alicia meant *exactly* when she said, "See you around, Joey" when they bumped into one another at The Gap.

"'See you around?'" Joey said. "See me around where? At school? Or was she hinting at something more? Does that mean she likes me? She wants to see *more* of me? It must, because I don't see her that much at school. Only twice a week in art class and even in there, we don't sit near one another, so she can barely see me. I think she wants me to call her. Take her out. Right, Jenni? That's what she's implying?"

I was the one who nodded along when he was trying to figure out what Claire was getting at when she said, "I wish my boyfriend was more like you, Joey" and hugged him hard enough that her breasts pushed up against him.

"It was a full-frontal hug, Jenni!" Joey said. "Not a side hug. You know there's a difference, right? She wanted me to feel them. She was definitely letting me know that if she were single she'd be all over me. I'm positive that's what she meant. Don't you agree? I should call her."

I was the one he cried to when Amanda broke his heart —for the third time.

"I love her so much! Why does she keep doing this to me?" he wailed as I fed him ice cream and resisted telling him that Amanda was a skank and he deserved better. I couldn't tell him that because he and Amanda had had an on-again off-again relationship since eighth grade and it would be on-again by the end of the month and soon I'd be forced to hang out with Amanda once again.

When Amanda moved on permanently and Joey was ready to get back out there and find a new girlfriend, I was the one who wrote the script for what he should say on the phone to woo his next leading lady. He needed so much help in that department. I would argue that is where I proved to be most valuable. Can you believe that before me, he actually started out his phone calls with "Whatchu doing, girl?" No, no, no, no! He was so lucky to have me. He even said so once.

"What would I do with out you, Jenni?" Joey slurred one night, drunk on Boone's Farm and loneliness. Amanda had made it quite clear that they were never ever ever getting back together again and Alicia had flatly turned him down when he asked her out after art class that afternoon.

My heart skipped a beat. I had watched way too many eighties teen romances where the unassuming, "plain" girl (usually played by a really beautiful actress in a pony tail and glasses) nabs the clueless hunk who just can't see that what he desired was in front of him the whole time! I was positive that was what was happening. (Even though I wasn't a stunner with a ponytail and four eyes.) *This is it,* I thought. *The moment I've been waiting for!*

"I don't know," I whispered, wishing I had glasses—even non-prescription ones!—he could remove, revealing my true hidden beauty. Tortoise shell ruins everyone's face! "What *would* you do?"

"You're the best, Jenni," Joey mumbled and closed his eyes. Soon he was snoring softly.

His words sent me into a tizzy. *The best? The best?!* What did that even mean? What was I supposed to surmise from that cryptic message?! The best at what? Was he trying to tell me more? Was he saying that maybe I'm the best ... thing that ever happened to him and he's realized he's in love with me and we should be together forever? Or was he saying maybe I'm the best ... friend he's ever had and he knows he can pass out drunk in my basement and I'd never rat him out? He knew I'd make up some elaborate cover story and his perfect image would remain untouched. I wanted to shake him awake and make him explain himself. But I didn't, because I was a scaredy-cat. I couldn't handle the truth. It was better to live in my dream world. I should have just asked for clarification, though, because I made myself crazy over the next several weeks. I found myself waking up in the night and thinking about his words: *What would I do without you? You're the best!* They filled me with hope and made me fantasize about the day Joey would finally come to his senses and see that I was the one for him.

Joey wasn't clueless. He knew I had a crush on him. And he used it to his advantage. Oh, don't worry, I didn't sleep with him or anything. But I did fan his ego like a motherfucker. I followed him around like a puppy dog. If he called, I dropped everything and cleared my schedule for him. Not that I was so busy, but I was busy enough. And sometimes I even avoided making plans, because he'd hinted that maybe—just maybe—he wanted to get together. So, I'd sit home alone by the phone and wait for it to ring. When he was feeling down he'd come over to my house and flop on the couch and start lamenting about how none of the girls at school liked him.

"They all think I'm a dork!" he said.

"You're not a dork!" I cried, rushing to his side where I commenced to blow a fuck-ton of sunshine up his (perfect) ass.

He pitted me against whatever girl he was seeing. The three of us would get together and he'd drop private jokes on us. I must admit, I did get a thrill when I'd see his girl-friend's cheeks flame and eyes narrow when she realized Joey and I shared a lot more secrets than the two of them. I'm not proud of my behavior but it was the one small joy I got. Remember, during these days I was always devastated because Joey was squiring some dumb, giggly ball of hair around town and I was stuck at home eating my weight in Cheetos. I was depressed and seeing his girlfriends irritated was a small sliver of happiness in my bleak, black world.

I let this behavior continue for longer than I should have. I let Joey lead me around like a brainless dolt, feeding his insatiable ego while completely depleting my own self-confidence in the process. I was, in a word, pathetic. But I couldn't stop. I'd think, *Today is the day that I cut Joey out of my life. He's a cancer and he needs to go.* And then he'd stop by my house and offer to take me to the movies.

The thought of sitting in a dark theater for two hours next to Joey was something I could never say no to. I was positive that everyone we passed thought he was my handsome boyfriend and it made me proud and gave me the confidence I was so desperately lacking. Plus, I was certain that at some point during the movie our hands would meet in the popcorn bucket and he'd feel the *zing* of desire. I prayed for him to put his arm around in my one of those fake stretch moves—or even if he needed a real stretch, his arm was still around me, that totally counted!

It was apparent Joey would have to do something pretty fucked up for me to finally put my foot down and tell him to get lost and find another loser to milk the life from. That day finally came in the spring. It was prom season and everyone was jittery. For once Joey didn't have a serious girlfriend and I really thought maybe there was a chance for me. I'd given up on the whole removing my glasses and seeing my inner/outer beauty thing, but I was still holding out for the my best friend is my dream girl scenario and what better place for it play out than prom? I was working up the nerve to prom-posal him before I even knew that was a thing. I was thinking of sending a pizza to the lunch room at school with "PROM?" spelled out in pepperoni. I was so ahead of my time! But I had a fear of public rejection, so I decided it would be better if I casually suggested we go to prom together. I worked on my speech for awhile and in the end it came out like, "Hey Joey, if you're not going to prom with anyone else, we should totally go together. That would be hilarious. Right?" I watched his face and died a little inside every second he hesitated. I was thinking, *Please go with me to prom and fall in love with me when you see me in my ah-may-zing dress.*

"That's a good idea," Joey agreed.

Wait. What???? I could barely contain my excitement.

"Only it's still early. Someone might ask you, Jenni. I'd hate for you to waste your time on me when there's someone better."

I was confused. What the fuck did that mean? Had there ever been anyone interested in me? What was he talking about? Was he trying to push me off with some jacked up backhanded compliment? Was he giving me that, "It's not you, Jenni, it's me" kind of thing? Surely not! I scrambled for an answer. "Well, I can't think of anyone I want to go with," I said. "I just thought it would be cool if we went together. No pressure and all that, y'know?"

"Oh, I know. It's a great idea," he said. "But let's just wait a bit and see, though. If we both don't have dates the week before, we should totally go together."

I breathed a sigh of relief. "Yeah, totally," I said.

"You're the best, Jenni."

A couple weeks later he called me and said, "I've been thinking about prom."

"Oh yeah?" I said, trying to be calm. "Is that coming up soon?"

Joey chuckled. "You really are funny, Jenni. It's, like, next week."

"Oh, wow. That was fast. Okay," I said, nervously. Inside I was like, *Holy shit, here we go. He's going to ask me to prom right now. Where can I find a dress at such late notice? I need something flattering but cool. I need to get my hair done. And my make up. This is going to cost a fortune, but Mom won't mind, she likes Joey. She's rooting for us.*

"So, I was thinking ..."

"Yeah ..." I said, barely breathing.

"Never mind," Joey said, abruptly.

"Wait. What?" I said, trying not to freak out. "What is it?"

"Well, this might be a lot to ask," he said.

"Try me," I said. I licked my lips. My mouth was so dry. I was so nervous.

"Well, prom's in a week. Did anyone ask you yet?"

My stomach flip-flopped. "Not that I know of," I said, giggling.

"Oh, that's too bad," Joey said.

"It's okay, I have a back up plan," I said.

"You do?" he asked. He sounded surprised.

"Umm ... yeah, I think so," I said. *YOU! You, dummy. You are my back up plan!*

"Well, that's great news," Joey said.

I was utterly and completely confused at that point. I decided it was time to be brave and cut through the bullshit and just say what I had to say instead of trying to read between the lines. "Joey, what did you call for?"

"Oh, right. Okay. So, prom's in a week..."

"Yes."

"And I have to ask you something..."

"Do it," I said.

He took a deep breath. "It's a pretty big ask. I should just get it over with," he said.

I stayed silent.

"Okay, here goes, do you think I can borrow your mom's car?"

I felt all of the air let out me. I literally deflated. "My mom's car?" I asked. My mom had a fancy convertible and no one—NO ONE—was allowed to drive it except for her. My parents made a big deal they couldn't afford to have me insured to drive it and so I had never even driven it. Joey knew this, so I wondered why he would ask to borrow her car? "Why?"

"I'm taking Stacy to prom and I can't afford a limo and I thought your mom's sweet convertible would be perfect. It would be so cool if Stacy and I showed up in that car."

It took every fiber of my being to not scream, "ARE YOU FUCKING KIDDING ME??????????????????"

Instead I said (quite calmly, actually—go, me!), "You're taking Stacy to prom?"

Stacy was a friend of ours. She was fairly quiet and mousy. She wore her hair in a ponytail and she had glasses.

He laughed self-consciously. "Yeah, I've been hanging out with her a lot. Did I not tell you that?"

"No, you've never mentioned it," I said. "Like, ever!"

"Yeah, we've been going to the movies and stuff. She's kind of quiet but she's really cool once you get to know her. I just didn't realize it until this week. When she asked me to prom, I was like, Yeah, why wouldn't I go to prom with her?"

"Why wouldn't you go to prom with her?" I asked. I fought to keep the hysteria from my voice.

"Yeah?"

"How about because we agreed to go together if we didn't get dates?"

"Right, we did say that. But then I got a date," Joey said, as if that cleared up everything.

"And now you want to take Stacy in my mom's convertible?"

"Yeah," he said. "Do you think she'll say yes?"

"Are you serious right now?" I asked.

I could hear him shrug. He was such a fucking idiot. No, *I* was the fucking idiot. At that moment I realized what a complete and total piece of shit Joey was. First, he agreed to go with me to prom ONLY if he couldn't find someone better and then he chose a girl who was only slightly better than me and then he asked to borrow my mom's car!! I wanted to break something—preferably Joey's cute face.

"Come on, Jenni. Your mom loves me," Joey said. "I bet she'll say yes."

"I bet she'll tell you to go fuck yourself and my mom never swears," I said.

Joey was stunned. "What the hell? Why are you so angry?"

"If you can't figure it out, I can't help you," I said. "Goodbye, Joey."

I hung up the phone and stormed off to find my mom—and large amounts of chocolate.

I filled her in on the Joey/Stacy saga with a lot of hand-wringing, tears, lamenting, cursing, and sugar. Just as I finished, the phone rang.

"Hello?" she said. She listened for a moment and mouthed "Joey" at me, raising an eyebrow. Her eyes narrowed and then she said, "Listen Joey, I don't know if you're heartless or clueless, but either way you don't deserve my daughter or my car. Find someone else to use!" She hung up the phone with a definitive *click.*

"What did he want?" I asked.

"What do you think?" she said. "He asked to borrow my car. I know you think he's smart, Jenni, but that kid doesn't have the brains he was born with. Good riddance."

I didn't go to the prom that year. Joey and Stacy went to prom and then he dumped her about a week later to get back together with Amanda who had reconsidered her never ever ever getting back together stance. Of course Amanda dumped him after the summer, but I wasn't there to stroke his hair and tell him that he was special. I was completely done with him.

This week I looked up Joey on Facebook. It made me more than a little happy to see he's still single. Yeah, yeah, I realize he could be single by choice, but that's not fun.

I like to think he's still single because he's an asshole.

NOTE FROM THE AUTHOR

Thank you for reading this collection. I appreciate your support and I hope you enjoyed it. I also hope you will tell a friend—or thirty about this. Please do me a huge favor and leave me a review on Amazon and Goodreads. Of course I prefer 5-star, but I'll take what I can get. If you hated this book, you can skip the review. *Namaste.*

ABOUT THE AUTHOR

Jen Mann is the hilarious *New York Times* best-selling author of *People I Want to Punch in the Throat: Competitive Crafters, Drop Off Despots, and Other Suburban Scourges* as well as several anthologies and short collections. Her books are inspired by her immensely popular blog People I Want to Punch in the Throat. Jen lives in Kansas with the Hubs and her two children, Gomer and Adolpha—no, those aren't their real names, their real names are actually worse. Jen spends her free time crafting and volunteering with the PTO. Seriously. Find Jen on social media and join her 1 million + fans.

Facebook: Jen Mann, People I Want to Punch in the Throat, I Just Want to Pee Alone, My Lame Life, LadyBalls

Twitter: @throat_punch

Instagram: @piwtpitt

Email: jenthroatpunch@gmail.com

www.peopleiwanttopunchinthethroat.com

www.jenmannwrites.com

ALSO BY JEN MANN

Working with People I Want to Punch in the Throat: Cantankerous Clients, Micromanaging Minions, and Other Supercilious Scourges

People I Want to Punch in the Throat: Competitive Crafters, Drop-off Despots, and Other Suburban Scourges

Spending the Holidays with People I Want to Punch in the Throat: Yuletide Yahoos, Ho Ho Humblebraggers, and Other Seasonal Scourges

———

My Lame Life: Queen of the Misfits

———

You Do You!

But Did You Die?

I Just Want to Be Perfect

I Still Just Want to Pee Alone

I Just Want to Be Alone

I Just Want to Pee Alone

Made in the USA
Columbia, SC
18 March 2020

89476470R00112